SOIL
2017

Notes Towards the
Theory and Practice
of Nurture Capital

Woody Tasch

SOIL: Notes Towards the Theory and Practice of Nurture Capital
Woody Tasch

Printed and bound in The United States of America
First printing, October 2017

Published by Slow Money Institute

Slow Money Institute
1035 Pearl Street, Suite 428
Boulder, Colorado 80302
www.slowmoney.org

Distributed in The United States by Chelsea Green Publishing

ISBN 978-0-692-93785-3

Colophon

Book Design	Cast Iron Design
Print & Bindery	D&K Printing
Paper	Neenah Conservation 100% PCW Recycled
Typography	GT SECTRA designed by Dominik Huber, Marc Kappeler, Noël Leu
	ROBINSON designed by Greg Gazdowicz

To Anne and Jack, Barbara and Eliot, Rose and Brook,
Jill and Eric, Kena and Mark, Michael and Kyle, Narendra,
Tomboy CFO, Nefertiti Hippie Piglet, Crescent Dragonwagon,
and John Maynard Keynes

If it's true that we are what we eat,
may it also be true
that we are not what we tweet.

Contents

Note to The Reader

I'm sad as hell and I'm not going to fake it anymore.

Our democracy is ebbing and carbon is flowing—into the atmosphere, that is, instead of back into the soil, where it belongs.

I'm sad as hell and I'm not going to forsake it anymore—poetry, that is.

To be sure, quirky, playful poetry is an idiosyncratic response to hundred-billion-dollar arms deals, nuclear uncertainty, a quadrillion dollars' worth of derivatives, hunger, obesity, and the invasion of every facet of life by media and markets. But, when I went looking for a meaningful response to the fakery of our current predicament, poetry is what I found.

Turns out that while you can't make this shit up and the truth is stranger than fiction, someone really did make this shit up, history is a nightmare from which we really do need to awake, and poetry may be truer than the realest news.

* * * * *

This is a call to farms. A call to all who plant, grow, harvest, eat, hug, argue, clink, put up, squirrel away, fritter away, lay away, and otherwise regret that civility and community went *that-a-way*. A call to gather our wits—one farm at a time, one town at a time, one county at a time, one watershed at time, one refusal to argue about politics at a time, one sleeve rolled up at a time.

Just why is it, anyway, that the economy keeps growing, military spending keeps exploding, drug prices keep soaring, the stock market keeps lifting off, but the strength of our marriages, the health of our kids, the vitality of our Main Streets, and the fertility of our soil keep going down?

My search for answers, encouraged by conversations with thousands of folks around the country, leads me to explore the boundaries between heart and mind, between finance and poetry, between fiduciary responsibility and free-range imagination.

* * * * *

Is the sky really falling this time? It has fallen before—after the Holocaust and Hiroshima, the assassinations of JFK, RFK, and MLK, the war in Vietnam, Kent State, Watergate, Black Monday, Enron, 9/11, Shock and Awe, Bernie Madoff, the Great Recession. Now, in the second decade of the 21st century, climate change, terrorism, widening wealth inequality, and fake news are clamping down on our consciousness. We need to discover new ways to bend entropy, befuddlement, and violence towards beauty, health, and peace.

That's what bunches of us have been doing, in very small ways, since 2009, in tents, barns, theaters, performing arts centers, farmers markets, restaurants, and other gathering spots in scores of communities around the country (and a few in Canada, France, and Australia), under the loose banner of Slow Money. More than $57 million has gone to over 600 small, organic food enterprises. Yes, we are putting a little of our money into local food systems. But what is driving us forward is something more—an impulse towards beauty, health, and peace.

There is also a more basic impulse. It's the impulse to be real neighbors, rather than fake neighbors—fake meaning our cars are parked here, our kids are in school here, we shop here, our roofs are pounded by the same hailstorms, but most of our money is doing god knows what god knows where, our political energies are swallowed up by national and international shenanigans, and our bonds as community members are wanting.

* * * * *

As this volume was being put to bed, Richard Haass, President of the Council on Foreign Relations, stated, "We just have to face the fact that our government isn't working." Add to this what Nobel laureate Joseph Stiglitz said a few years back, "We aren't fixing the structural problems of the economy because we don't know what the structural problems are."

We sense that macroeconomic fixes and national political debates are not enough. We sense that what we are being fed is not healthy. We sense that our cultural compass is no longer reliable. Which is why we are all going a little bit crazy right now.

If we are going to change course, really and truly change course, we must start by standing our ground against things dumbed down, watered down, twittered down, trickled down, and hunkered down, against things overly politicized, polemicized, marginalized, externalized, rationalized, systematized, professionalized, fiscalized, intellectualized, and anti-intellectualized.

In this pursuit, I've gone Poetically Incorrect, because I harbor the suspicion that deep down, deeper down than the Ogallala Aquifer and the deepest recesses of fear, millions of us can still find the wherewithal to allow rhyme to flirt with reason in the land of the free and the home of the peaceably inclined.

W.T.

Part One

Poetically Incorrect

Invocation

Oh, gods and goddesses! *Oh, demigods and quasi-deities! Oh, ether breathers and prayer receivers, heavenly custodians of the hereafter and downward dogs of the here and now, Holy Ones and wisdom keepers, Northern seers and Southern sages, Eastern gurus and Western priests, muses and metaphysicians! Sing in us a song of life after fast food and fast money, fast information and fast technology, fast change and faster change! Bring blessed pause to all the poor, rich, bewildered peoples of these Great Accelerating Anthropocene Proceedings! Come out, come out, wherever you are! We have questions to toss into the fire: Where were you when we cultivated wheat? Where were you when the cube was Rubiked? Where were you when the arc of history turned into a Great Exponential Curve, as if there were no end? Enough already with your pantheistic laissez-faire shenanigans! Let's raise our glasses! Here's to fermentation! Here's to anything that rhymes with divine and wine and moonshine and Einstein! Here's to life after high fructose corn syrup and CAFOs and GMOs, aging plutonium nuke triggers, driverless cars and Mars missions, Dead Zones and Twilight Zones, clever phones and puzzled pheromones, and orchards full of almond trees awaiting swarms of robobees!*

Oh, earthworms! *Oh, Lumbricidae and actinomycetes and mycorrhizae, nematodes and tardigrades, dung beetles and millipedes! Oh, harbingers of fertility, humus healers and tilth tenders, myriad keepers of decomposition and microbial denizens of the soil! Where were you when making a living became making a killing? Where were you when farms became factories?*

Oh, moneylenders! *Oh, silo tenders and spice traders! Oh, stockholders, entrepreneurial spirits and economists, makers of booms and busts, exchangers of goods and services, investors and fiduciaries, Moonshot Takers and Unicorn Makers, profiteers extraordinaire and decriers of usury! Where were you when millions turned to billions and billions to trillions? Where were you when wampum turned into gold and gold into paper and paper into information and information into data and data into algorithms and algorithms into derivatives? And where will you be when Gaussian Copula Formula finally banishes Risk from all securities?*

A spot 4.7 miles (as the magpie flies) northeast of Devil's Thumb, several hours before the Imagination Tenders' arrival.

Devil's Thumb

I "I don't have that much sympathy for them," Jumbo Goddamn Mumbo
offered, his face aglow in the waning sun's orange-golden rays.
Pigments of Yoruba, Kahina, Creole, Arapaho, Apache, and Yaqui
lent his youthful visage tints of ancient struggles and ageless ways.
(Family lore suggested there was also some Caledonian in the mix,
courtesy of the Sand Creek massacre, although to discover any hints
of northern European lineage in this countenance one would need
to summon powers of discernment as great as those of Georgescu-Roegen,
who right at that moment was pausing in his analysis of our entropic fix,
the future of natural systems, and the efficacy of various economic tricks
to study the last few drops of Laphroaig in Rogue Algorithm's glass.)

He stooped, cupped his hands and brought the frigid water to his lips.
"It has only been a few generations and already our language is lost.
Too many peaks with names like Yankee Doodle, Jasper, Gray's, Rollins,
Bald, and Moffatt. Honoring European settlers is one thing, but..."

Mamma Mumbo walked towards him holding out a loaf of bread.
"Me dear, dear nephew. Can't be changin' history. But got to eat.
Babettes Pain Natural—beyond de' beyond, *n'est-ce pas?*"

II "The place where water flows in two directions?" Estcheemah guessed.
She had listened well all those years to Night Bear, Sweet Water,
and Green Fire Mouse, learning never to accept the old teachings as rote.

"You mean you don't actually know what the ancestors called this place?"
Fukuoka asked, brimming with incredulity, concern, and skeptical delight.
"There's knowing and there's knowing," Sweet Water's half-descendant replied.

"Let's Google it," Glitch quipped, his usual insouciance on display.

Then two-minded Zeuss joined in, his real intent only partly showing.
"We're not here for idle chatter. We're here to consider a weighty matter."

"Not all that weighty," Hermes said with a smirk.
"Just another in a long line of mankind's meshuggeneh invocations."

III   "Venus is smiling upon us," Zero Chief noted, looking southwest.

Their attention went skyward, as if no invitation were needed.
Demigods, minor deities, quasi-mythical characters, each flirting
with immortality in his or her own way, plus a few souls so steeped
in cryptic enthusiasm that it was almost otherworldy—
this was not a crew that was inclined to wait for an invitation.
Perhaps the evening's first star should be wishing on *them...*

A dimple shown near the sliver moon's oblique smile,
blessing the peaks without the slightest trace of guile.

"Venus, shmenus," Jumbo Goddamn Mumbo snorted.
"Are we going to try to help them or not?"

IV   Flow of light, flow of memory past night, towards and away
and back again, past dream, past volition's coming and contrition's
going, past early and late, past church and state, past stream,
past consciousness, past fear of darkness and dread of suspicion.

Flow of particle, flow of wave, flow of supernova born,
flow of creation's imperative, towards and away and back again,
ought and naught, ceaseless expansion and inevitable contraction,
black hole's attraction, myth's embrace, glimmers of galactic origin.

A little before moonrise.

V   Every peak, every steep slope, every crevice, every alpine meadow,
every stream, every river, every canal, every aquifer, every well, every
reservoir, every water right bought and sold, every indication of depletion,
every droughty projection, every gutter, every rain barrel, every story
ever told about irrigation, cultivation, civilization—

  it was all too much
to keep track of, even for them. Even for Moolah Mullah, who had forgotten
more about inventory and accounting than any of them would ever know.

Every balance sheet, every double entry, every ledger, every abacus bead,
every decimal, every dividend, every royalty, every temple scroll,
every tax, every tithe, every bit of capital ever gained, every receipt,
every arithmetic concept, every tally ever tallied, every stock market
ever rallied, every fourth ever sallied, every dalliance ever dallied—

Calculus and Aphrodite
The Lowly and the Mighty
Cattail and Phragmite
Profitability and Infinity
Fertility and Salinity
Imagination and Decay
Come What and May—

It wasn't easy, but Moolah Mullah emptied his head of it all.

VI To the likes of Tethys, Varuna, Lethe, Liffey, Putumayo, Snohomish,
Colorado, and Mississippi, a few incantations were offered, without much fuss.

Then, not quite yet time for their deliberations to begin,
Zero Chief stirred the pot. "I have a question," he said.

"Not another of your faux zen koans," Glitch groaned.
"More a Quaker query, I'd like to think," Zero Chief replied.

The non sequitur-loving sachem squatted unceremoniously
atop a boulder of biotite gneiss, his haunches haunching
as only the haunches of a cypher-doting sachem could.
Ancient, but definitely not past its prime, his presence was nothing
if not partially sublime. Naught negation draped about him,
as unmistakable as it was invisible. His bearing had about it a certain
alienated majesty. The tilt of his head, his gaze, his aura—all hinted
at the post-modern, pre-post-whatever-was-next wisdom that was about
to be minted. You didn't need to be a hedge fund manager to sense it.

The slab on which he perched further enhanced this impression—
so startlingly symmetrical, cuboid, and remarkably rectangular

that it would have been at home in pyramid, temple, monument, Carcassonne parapet, or jumbled crop of toppled Inca sarsen.

From this vantage, the symbol-savoring sage asked, anxious to turn their attention to the convening's purpose:

"Is philanthropy the run-off of a broken system?"

It would have seemed a rather strange question to any but those to whom it had been posed, which was, of course, the very reason it was they and no others who had been asked to assemble. Yet, tired and exhilarated from their journeys, they were not ready to dip their sacred toes into such treacherous, secular waters. Symbiosis was still gathering firewood. Zahuah stretching. Radius distracted by geometries of a more symmetrical nature.

"A most interesting notion," Moolah Mullah surprised them all, taking Zero Chief's question to heart.

"And not without historical implications. The Northwest Palace at Nimrud was renowned for its water catchment system, although there was no mention of water in the accounting of King Assurnasirpal's philanthropy. A certain generosity could, I suppose, be ascribed to the palace's lavish celebratory dedication:

> 'For ten days I gave them food, I gave them drink, I had
> them bathe, and I had them anointed. Thus, did I honor
> them and send them back to their lands in peace and joy.'

Cuneiform on an Assyrian orthotast from the palace of King Assurnasirpal II in Nimrud. Cuneiform used a base 60 notation system, whence derive 60 minutes in an hour and 60 seconds in a minute and 360 degrees in a circle.

"It was 876 BCE. From all over Assyria, 69,574 invitees arrived. They enjoyed 1,500 ducks, 500 geese, 10,000 turtle doves, 10,000 loaves of bread, 10,000 jugs of beer, 10,000 skins of wine, and great quantities of lamb, nuts, spices, dates, and vegetables. Those were the days when a silver shekel got you 234 liters of barley, 270 liters of dates, 66 liters of sesame, and 18 liters of olive oil. Prices were volatile, however. The Tariff Stela indicates that the king was quite concerned about fluctuating exchange rates."

"Someone mention Quakers?" Mamma Mumbo interjected.
"Dey love me apple pie!"

It is doubtful that any Quaker had ever experienced
the glories of her apple pie with its famous cheddar crust.
But ending such historical pecuniary banter, before it got
out of hand, was, to her thinking, an absolute must.

VII   Big Thompson, Boulder, Horsetooth, Barker, Silver, Gold, Left Hand,
Cache Le Poudre, St. Vrain, Beckwith, Rough & Ready, Oligarchy,
Palmerton, Farmers' High Line, People's, South Platte, North Platte,
Platte, Missouri—
                    a great downward journey, an endless dendritic
drainage from the Continental Divide southeastward through the foothills
towards the Great Plains and then the Greater Oceans beyond,
born (not really born, since, according to geologists and hydrologists
and echohydrologists and hydrometeorologists and ecologists, it's billions
of years old and constantly cycling) in innumerable places such as these,
outcroppings and ravines such as these, snowmelt, trickles and drips,
seeps and gradients and springs, tiny confluence and small tributary,
through gully and glade, meander and oxbow, floodplain and canyon,
pool and shoal and shallow. At the headwaters
our wee band of Imagination Tenders
gathered, as wide-eyed as Newton
savoring his first *tarte tatin*
or gypsies at a ticker tape
parade.

VIII   Reverie-friendly Night shook a few more stars from her cloak.

Jumbo Goddamn Mumbo, Zero Chief, Glitch, Estcheemah and the others
sat around the fire, krummholz branches and twigs of limber pine
burning in a small pit. Sparks leapt joyously up into the dusk.
*What laws of nature? How climate change? Why fractals? Where does a
mountain weigh? And why was it that Demeter wasn't speaking
to Ashanti?*

(None of which was actually on their minds. So, as reverie-caressing Night
went about her customary duties, she had an easy time of it, tidying
up to the west, gathering her shroud, then slipping out of sight.)

IX   Every sacramental urge, every spiritual impulse, every transcendental
craving, every suggestion of exaltation, every search for communion,
every metaphysical speculation, every ontological suggestion,
every cloud of understanding, every drop
of possibility—
                    it was all there, a philosophical feast,
the gumbo of all gumbos, but only Glitch was hungry.

"Is it too late for more of those *refritos*?" he inquired.

From a small pouch that seemed special, Zero Chief removed
pieces of vellum and passed them around the circle, each
keeping one on which to write. Not since Valkyrie hovered
over the first experiments of Haber and Bosch had such a ritual
been attempted. (At that juncture, success had been limited, it's true,
but it just might be that the time had finally come for something new.)

Mamma Mumbo took the lead, the tips of her braids licked by the fire's
soothing glow. She closed her eyes, allowing what happens when you
close your eyes to happen, then looked down to the words she had
written and declared:

   This be de' recipe I never tasted.

As she spoke, she offered the vellum with care to the vigorous flames,
which received them with obvious gratitude, although not without
a certain degree of thermodynamic detachment. Reverie-inducing Night
drew her cloak a bit closer once more, as Zero Chief followed suit:

   This is the prayer I never uttered.

Glitch, Meme Warrior, Radius, Hermes, Zeuss, Zahuah, Symbiosis,
Rasputin, Estcheemah, Moolah Mullah, and Chiogga—each took their turn.

> *This is the data Rogue Algorithm spared.*
> *This is the phrase that never went viral.*
> *This is the circle that never got squared.*
> *This is the race I never ran.*
> *This is the rhyme that wasn't in time.*
> *This is the fatwa no Imam ever issued.*
> *This is the associative power that never gets old.*
> *This is the юродивый[1] I never quite became.*
> *This is the love Sweet Water offered.*
> *This is the interest no lender ever charged.*
> *This is the borscht no Jewish mother ever wasted.*

Then Fukuoka, courtesy of some pretty fancy impromptu origami,
contributed his own blessed two cents, in the shape of a tiny crane:

> *This is the knowledge that does us no good.*

Jumbo Goddamn Mumbo remained silent, not quite in a trance,
peering intently through Night's diaphanous veil, until they all
followed his glance towards a spot just above the tree line,
where, dimly, a small ephemeral commotion could be discerned.
They were Sapiens shades, dancing a clever, akimbo dance
of unrepentant curiosity and unbridled chance. In something of a hora
(or was it a kolo?), they went around, looking alternately to the heavens
and to the ground, singing, each in their own tongue—Urdu, Aramaic, Maghrebi,
Mandarin, Linux, Escheri, Nowwhatl, Swahili, Gaelic, Castilian, and Idiazabal—
a chorus neither haunting nor lilting, as sacredly cacophonous as it was inane:

> *This is the homework God ate.*
> *This is the seed we did not save.*
> *This is the peace we could not make.*
> *This is the place we would not inhabit.*

Jumbo Goddamn Mumbo almost spoke, but thought better of it.

---

[1] Pronounced yurodivy. Russian for the Eastern Orthodox Church's "Holy Fool."

X They sat for a few hours, warming themselves in silence.
The Continental Divide seemed insignificant, now, compared
with that to which they were bearing witness: the divide
between history and possibility, between man's heart and his head.

Then with and without words, they weighed the weightiest of factors—
the future of myth, the now of technology, the advent of the virtual,
the distortion of belief, the half-life of fact, the proliferation of information,
the fragility of civility, the off-shoring of manufacturing, carbon
and carbon sinks, calories in soft drinks, toxins in the smallest amounts,
Fibonacci's spiral, God's death, Gaia's breath, Dan and Daphne's garlic,
and the need to change the passwords on Georgescu-Roegen's gmail accounts.

Every ethical entreaty, every primitive suspicion, every tribal antipathy,
every epiphany, every encyclical, every bit of doctrine, every law
(theological, economic, scientific, and otherwise), every bit of universal
empathy, every shred of political nobility—
                                        all were being tossed
into the fire of human progress, producing great quantities of light and
heat, but at what cost? Across the planet, intentions (best, better, good,
and otherwise) kept pouring out, unrelenting and persistent as plumes
from the smokestacks of corporate faith and industrial doubt—
ghost cities of intention, warehouses full of intentions, farm fields
emptied of intentions, aquifers depleted of intention, memories
whose intention had been to hold their own against the Great Quickening,
Cracker Jack boxes hiding little trinkets of intention, intention fracked
and spent, Wall Street traders shouting intentions with an urgency that belied
the implacable, pale non-demeanor of the Great Fiduciary in the Sky—
our intrepid cadre of Imagination Tenders breathed it all in, here,
high up where the earth ends and the sky begins, where apple's dream
of pie gets a little woozy, where the air is thinner than the pope's hair,
and where, before they could coax out of the ether any consensus about whether,
somehow, against all odds, they might be able to help mankind change course,
Mamma Mumbo suddenly found herself saying, without a hint of remorse,

"Yo, Glitch. Those *refritos* be long gone."

The Milky Way over Brainard Lake
(Bo Insogna)

XI   They had the universe's number.

It wasn't 3.14159265358979323846264338327950288419716939937510058
20974944592307816406286208998628034825342117067982148086513
28230664709384460955058223172535940812848111745028410270193
85211055596446229489549303819644288109756659334461284756482
33786783165271201909145648566923460348610545326648213393 6072
60249141273724587006606315588174881520920962829254091715 3643
678925903600113305305488204665213841469519415116009...

No matter if you took it to an ungodly number of places.
A billion. A quadrillion. That wasn't it. (Although a googol,
if spelled with the utmost correctness, might be a plex
of a different color. Milky Way white, perhaps.)

In the end of the beginning was the number.

They knew that. As surely as they knew the difference
between Venus and Shmenus.

XII   It was a certain quotient of affection they were after.

There was no formula. Or was there? If there was
a recipe for disaster—and obviously there was that—
then surely there must be a quotient of affection.
Or was it up to them to see that one survived?

Emotional numerator, meet intellectual denominator.
Spiritual ruminator, meet psychological calibrator.
Maslovian compunction, meet meta-economic function.
Imagination's reduction, meet innuendo's conjunction.

Innuendo is your beginningo.

11:59:59.	*Square root of Shakespeare minus length of dousing rod.*
Then.	*Zeno's fraction over Moebius' strip.*
Now.	*The time it takes a grip to slip.*
256.	*The distance between truth and power.*
128.	*Gallons per second.*
64.	*Degrees of difficulty.*
32.	*Parts per million.*
16.	*The speed of darkness.*
8.	*Angels on the head of a pin.*
4.	*The weight of the world on their shoulders.*
2.	*The specific gravity of America and Boulder.*

A few dashes of hastemakeswaste. Essence of doesn'taddup. Pinch of takeaway.
Ground caraway to taste. Dusting of flowerpower. A few buds that've been nipped.
And under no circumstances whatsoever must any kombucha ever be sipped
anywhere near these gastronomic premises. Nor the word probiotic spoken.
Nor any answers from artificial intelligence supplied. Nor neither implied.
Wonder under. Zero in. Figure out. Boil down. Rustle up. Catch on. Nod off.

It was a certain quotient of affection they were after.

The rarefied mountain air was still, mysterious, clear, humbling, and subtle,
with apparently boundless capacity to accept whatever they might tender—
earnest banter, occasional cries of despair, the fertile babble of good will,
and, last but not least, more than a little good-natured laughter.

XIII "Is it true that Darwin spent the last years of his life
observing earthworms?" Estcheemah wondered aloud, asking
a question to which someone might actually have an answer.
"Sitting here with all of you on this momentous occasion,
it seems most fabulous to think of him, the aging, British scientist,
weighing the earth ejected from a single burrow and measuring
earthworm castings per square foot, per square yard, and per acre."

"As fabulous as the presence of annelids in alpine meadows,"
Fukuoka observed, gesturing towards their immediate environs.

"How, my lowlands farm boy, do you happen to know anything
about earthworms in alpine meadows?" Glitch chided.

"I try to know as little as possible," Fukuoka replied. He paused,
allowing his words to percolate, then decided to share more.
"But I do know that even in the shadows of Chandra Parbat,
Kharchakund, Kalanag, and all those 20,000 ft. peaks,
the life of worms in Uttarkashi is remarkably similar
to that of worms on the hillsides overlooking Matsuyama Bay
and the broad Dogo Plain. The biologists of Nanda Devi
once regaled me with their taxonomy, and, for reasons I myself
shall never comprehend, nor wish to, it stayed with me like poetry—

    Lennogaster pusillus, Metaphire houlleti,
    M. anomala, Ocnerodrilus occidentalis,
    Dendrodrilus rubidus, Aporrectodea calliginosa,
    Amynthas corticis, Drawida nepalensis—

sweeter to my ears than any prayer, just why I cannot say."

Glitch's thoughts drifted from the meadows below Jasper Lake
to the pastures near Lanweilaha Mountain in Yushu province,
where the golden worm is foraged for its medicinal properties.
(It isn't actually a worm, but rather a fungus-infested caterpillar larva—
yartsa gunbu, they call it—worth more than its weight
in gold. The last time he had been there, a yak herder had invited
him into her tent, where, beneath a picture of the Dalai Lama,
she took a yellow cloth off of a small box and opened it to reveal
a dozen or so intact specimens of *yartsa gunbu*.)

Yartsa Gunbu

Hermes' thoughts drifted back towards other treasures,
towards the Golden Age, towards his long-lost Olympian kin,
towards rosy-fingered dawn over Ithaka and Circe's cave
and the Laestrygonians, towards the Lavrion mines, whose silver,
into tetradrachms made, financed the swift triremes
that turned back the Persians at the straits of Salamis.
(It was silver, as well, onto which a wing`ed visage, mistaken
for his, would one day be forged. Did the wings on Liberty's cap
betoken freedom of thought? Why the fasces and the battle axe atop,

olive branch nestled beside, as if to purchase both war and peace?
"Armed with a Mercury dime," a historian would one day write,
"youngsters in the 1940s had their choice of a 52-page comic book,
a double-dip ice cream cone, two Hershey bars, or two bottles of Coca-Cola.")
His thoughts, famous for being fleeting, next flew to Potosí, where,
in the days after Francisco Pizarro's arrival, the five great seams
of the Cerro Rico became the object of every conquistador's desire—
45,000 tons of silver transformed into bar and coin and shipped to Seville.

Hermes? Mercury? It is rumored that Adolph A. Weinman, the sculptor who designed this dime, used as a model Elise Stevens, the wife of poet Wallace Stevens. (It's no wonder he once wrote, "Money is a kind of poetry.")

(Had Moolah Mullah known what Hermes was thinking, he would
have added, "The Incas, whose empire was moneyless, called gold
the sweat of the sun and silver *the tears of the moon*.")

Zahuah, her demure demeanor betraying an urge for adventure,
shot a glance over her shoulder, then lowered her gaze once more.

Then sighed Symbiosis. North of thought and south of emotion,
her inner workings whirred. Echo traded stories with memory.
Whisper of sweet nothing exchanged secrets with mysterious attraction.
Everywhere, two sides were looking for no coin—root exudate and colloidal
cation, concentration and diffusion, ultra-biological infusion and subterranean
collusion, osmotic acceptance and conjugal embrace, last call and first impression,
mycorrhizal make believe and microbial commotion and then some,
all conspiring on fecundity's behalf, in earth as it is in humus,
overly mysterious and underly obvious and utterly pervious, as if,
from her right amygdala to left, a curious, fearless arbitrage of flight and fight,
after flowing for so many millennia, had suddenly ceased without a trace.

She sighed again, while Meme Warrior fumbled beside her with the flap
of his rucksack, festooned with the State Seal of Colorado. "Why the dictum
NIL SINE NUMINE—Nothing Without the Deity? Why the Masonic eye of God?
Why the fasces and mining tools, but no branding iron, no blasting cap?"

Chiogga was in his own world. Venezia and Castello 3303,
Beta maritima and fennel and the earth-smell of geosmin
all came to him, as his discernment slowed, flowing gently
from the tips of his root hairs to the tops of his ruby-veined greens.

Fukuoka's knowing was coming and going. His earthworm prayer
gave way to the daikon and rape flowers and rice straw at Shikoku.
"The ultimate goal of farming," he said aloud, "is not the growing
of crops, but the cultivation and perfection of human beings." [2]

2   *The One-Straw Revolution,* Masanobu
Fukuoka (Rodale Press, 1978) p. 119

XIV

Zero Chief surveyed the troops, whose varied visages displayed
a mix of dreamily inspired compassion and sublimated dismay.
They had known what was at hand when they'd agreed to gather.
They had known their ranks would be a bit bedraggled after all this time.
They knew the limits of their ability to intervene, even if a pattern
were to emerge that they all could see, much less a plausible
course of action upon which they all could concur. They knew
Aristotle's words, "That which is common to all is least cared for."
And the old saw, "Know how to make a million dollars farming?
Start with two." They knew the magic and mystery and science
of photosynthesis and transpiration and mitochondrial mischief.
They all would have shaken their heads, pretty much in unison,
at Da Vinci's prescience: "We know more about the movement
of the celestial bodies than the soil underfoot." They knew
that the journey from the Age of Agriculture to the Age of Information
had been swift, titillating, and inconclusive. They knew. As with so much
in mankind's cockamamie, ingenious agricultural journey, the imperative
to produce yet outweighed—consistently, efficiently, industriously, industrially—
the impulse to nurture. (Which is why they were all hanging on with such
ferocity to the idea that Earth was their Mother. What would be happening
if Earth were their Brother?) They knew who Ray Kroc was. They knew
the share price of McDonald's on the day of the ten billionth person.
They knew what was behind fiduciary exuberance of the irrational kind.
They knew why Zoë Bradbury prefers horses to tractors (and why
she's also quite fond of the old Ford 5000 she'd found up in Port Orford).
They knew why Wendell Berry had written each of his 48 books.
They knew the way wren looks at warbler and why the sky is blue.
They knew how easy it was to mistake fear for greed.
They knew the difference between mere want and desperate need.

They knew where all the swords and ploughshares were hidden.
They knew that someday somewhere someone somehow was going
to get up the nerve to say, "Don't ask. Don't till." Or something worse.
They got it. They understood. They felt it. They really did.

And they also knew this was serious. As serious as blank verse.

XV Which brings us to the crust of Babettes bread. This is a subject of considerable
interest among those lucky enough to have enjoyed it. Lucky, because it is
extremely crusty, caramelized, dark, even verging, some say, on burnt. It elicits
very strong reactions. Lucky, because it is expensive. Not the crust, the loaf.
$10. Even per pound (it's heavy), it's still pricey. The average cost of a U.S. loaf
in 2014 was $2.37 (ranking 21st globally, just below Jamaica at $2.44 and above
Ghana at $2.32). Moolah Mullah's attention had first been brought to this general
topic decades ago, when, during a meal at Henrietta's Table in Cambridge, he
had inquired of his waiter, Mamadou (who hailed from Senegal and had been
working at that restaurant in The Charles Hotel for many, many years), after
mentioning how much he relished the slices of walnut cranberry bread that
came with breakfast, as to the possibility of purchasing an entire loaf. After a
few minutes, Mamadou returned with the bad news: "$16.00." And that was in
2005. Could it be? What would it cost today? We should be afraid to ask. This
is, surely, the polar opposite of Wonder Bread. An expression of quality and
individuality to which large-scale commercial baking does not know how to affix
a value. $16.00 isn't a value. It's just a wildly high price. It's what happens when
the Invisible Hand throws its hand up, capitulates, throws in the towel, flings
the cloche to the floor in exasperation and storms out of the kitchen, muttering
about foodies and artisans and levain. No time for the Maillard reaction, as
it's known, the interactions of sugars, starches, and protein in a dark, crusty
crust, because, you see, not all crusts are created equal. The breadness of bread
(Thank You, Joel Salatin, for "the pigness of pigs" and so much more!) is not only
manifest in the crustiness of crust, but in all aspects of sourcing, milling, starting,
kneading, proofing, and baking. The type of wheat matters. The type of milling
matters. The speed of mixing matters. In the 1950s, the speed of electric millers
doubled, to around 80 revolutions a minute, driving more oxygen into the dough,
bleaching the carotenoids, and producing ever-whiter crumb. The kind of yeast,
and, in the case of sourdough, lactobacillus, matters. The amount of time devoted
to rising and fermentation matters. Temperature during proofing and baking

Not all crusts are created equal.

The first automatically sliced commercial loaves were produced on July 6, 1928, in Chillicothe, Missouri, using a machine invented by Otto Rohwedder. Wonder Bread brought sliced bread to the mass market in 1930.

matters. The kind of oven matters. Willingness to consider the possibilities of something called Roasted Onion and Asiago Miche might even matter. The Tassajara folks consider bread-making the way to an open heart. *What is this, a loaf of bread or performance art?* I'm just saying: There's a reason that Bethlehem is Hebrew for "house of bread." There's a reason money is referred to as dough (despite the fact that Hostess Brands, Wonder Bread's parent, declared bankruptcy in 2012). There's a reason that a Babettes loaf sells for what it sells for and that on Sunday mornings you have to get there by 10:00 a.m. if you want one. (Forensic analysis of the elitism suggested by discussions of the crustiness of crust and the cost of artisan loaves, as well as issues relating to gluten intolerance and the geopolitics of wheat exports, were not on the agenda of them that'd gathered near Devil's Thumb. Nor was the derivation of the names Wonder Bread and Devil's Thumb—lore attributing the latter to the cessation of hostilities between the Ute and Arapaho, although a convincing narrative was not easy to find.)

XVI

Every commodity price, every fluctuation, every speculation, every bet, every spread, every forward contract on a bushel of corn, every hog belly, every credit default swap, every ultra-high frequency trade, every tranche, every security sliced and diced into the rationality of the invisible investor, every Nikkei Index, every glycemic index, every ETF, every electron of entrepreneurship and productivity, every algorithmic glimpse into the vast inner workings of distant markets—

none of this seemed to matter for a brief instant, as 13 billion-year-old starlight reached them, greeted them, touched them, even cozied up to them, almost as if it were trying to speak. *Were they going to sit up all night? What would happen if they couldn't come to consensus? Would this be their last convening? Where were Georgescu-Roegen and Rogue Algorithm, anyway, and what exactly were they cooking up? Had anyone brought an extra Patagonia fleece? And what about the national debt of Greece?*

The moon, it appeared, was heading towards Jackson Hole.

They stirred, a bit bleary, a bit despondent, vaguely expectant, unwilling to give up. Chiogga wandered over towards the meadow's border. Zero Chief walked alone along the ridge. Zahuah and Glitch considered having a fling. (No one was aware, but at that very moment,

in a nook beneath a precipice beside a ledge above a perilous perch,
Hope was courting Inkling, even though they hadn't been invited.)
Moolah Mullah and Mamma Mumbo made their way towards the place
where the shades had danced, gesturing at turns wildly, at turns equivocally,
mimicking the seemingly eternal drama of this forgiving and that grace.

But only a native goddess sat in a lonely dream by the dark creek's flowing edge,
quietly weeping, but shrewd, and gently vowed to woo the next imagining.

END OF NIGHT ONE

Part Two

Imagination

I   **Whereabouts**

Imagination.

We can't all be Noam Chomsky or Ayn Rand or Wendell Berry or Bingo Pajama,[1] but that doesn't mean each and every one of us can't get the hint. We need a new story. Maybe even a new myth. We need to rediscover imagination.

Imagination that enables us to reckon our whereabouts in a world that is heating up and speeding up. Imagination that enables us to find our way past shallow punditry, tribal vitriol, global this and cyber that, past the hyper and the ultra and the mega. Imagination that leads us back to one another, to the places where we live, and to the land—not just the land of *"this land is your land, this land is my land,"* but also the soil itself, upon which all life depends.

Imagination.

My own journey in this direction has been catalyzed over the past decade by interactions with thousands of folks in Slow Money meetings, large and small, in dozens of communities.[2] It felt to me, at the outset, that we would do well to listen more to farmers and poets and less to CEOs and economists. Now, I'm ready to double down.

I'll see your tweets, your big data, your Dow Jones Industrial Average, your political outrage of the day, and raise you thousands of CSAs,[3] millions of organic beets, and a healthy dose of literary imagination, or, more specifically, some Thomas Mann, or, more specifically than that, some Hans Castorp, the protagonist in Mann's 1924 novel *The Magic Mountain*, which evoked Europe on the eve of the First World War. Surrounded by questions of civilization and decay, disease and health, Castorp has the epiphany of all epiphanies. Lost and exhausted in an Alpine snowstorm, it comes:

> *For the sake of goodness and love, man shall*
> *let death have no sovereignty over his thoughts.*[4]

1   Bingo Pajama is a character in Tom Robbins' novel *Jitterbug Perfume*. Bees live in his hair.

2   Slow Money is a movement sparked by *Inquiries into the Nature of Slow Money: Investing as if Food, Farms and Fertility Mattered* (Chelsea Green, 2008). For more, visit www.slowmoney.org.

3   CSA stands for community supported agriculture, a program through which farm customers pre-pay for a share of the season's produce.

4   *The Magic Mountain*, Thomas Mann (Alfred A. Knopf, 1985) p. 496

Castorp found himself in a fictional blizzard; today, we are lost in a blizzard of the virtual and the fake.

Try this: Where Castorp says death, substitute terrorism or Twitter or, even... Twinkies.

> *For the sake of goodness and love, man shall*
> *let terrorism have no sovereignty over his thoughts.*
>
> *For the sake of goodness and love, man shall*
> *let Twitter have no sovereignty over his thoughts.*
>
> *For the sake of goodness and love, man shall*
> *let Twinkies have no sovereignty over his thoughts.*

Imagination.

Summon it and see that the rancor and uncertainty of the day, which seem so unprecedented, are subject to broad arcs of history:

Agricultural Revolution	10,000 years ago
Ancient Greece	2,500 years ago
Europe Colonizes New World	500 years ago
American Revolution and the Invisible Hand[5]	250 years ago
Industrial Revolution	150 years ago
Tech Revolution and Population Explosion	50 years ago
400 ppm Carbon in the Atmosphere	1 year ago
22,000 Dow Jones Industrial Average	2017

Imagination.

Summon it and see that, all the technological wizardry and wealth creation notwithstanding, we are exempt from neither the laws of gravity nor the wisdom of mythology. The ancient Greeks gave us Icarus and Pandora's Box and we are still acting these myths out. We invented cars to get horse poop off city streets and now we've got carbon in the atmosphere. We deployed nuclear weapons as a deterrent and now we face proliferation and terrorism. We developed antibiotics and now we're dealing with antibiotic-resistant superbugs. We're empowered by Twitter and Facebook but we're losing the integrity of our elections. We're chasing the dream of terraforming Mars, but we can't figure out how to stem soil erosion in Iowa, rebuild Baltimore, or save Aleppo.

5   In 1776, Adam Smith's *An Inquiry into the Nature and Causes of the Wealth of Nations* put forth the concept of the invisible hand of the marketplace, whereby each individual pursuing his or her own gain contributes to the well being of all: "As every individual, therefore, endeavours as much as he can both to employ his capital in the support of domestic industry, and so to direct that industry that its produce may be of the greatest value; every individual necessarily labours to render the annual revenue of the society as great as he can. He generally, indeed, neither intends to promote the public interest, nor knows how much he is promoting it. By preferring the support of domestic to that of foreign industry, he intends only his own security; and by directing that industry in such a manner as its produce may be of the greatest value, he intends only his own gain, and he is in this, as in many other cases, led by an invisible hand to promote an end which was no part of his intention. Nor is it always the worse for the society that it was no part of it. By pursuing his own interest he frequently promotes that of the society more effectually than when he really intends to promote it." (Book Four, Chapter Two)

Imagination.

OK. I can't circle around this topic without citing Einstein:

"Imagination is more important than knowledge. Knowledge is limited. Imagination encircles the world."

(Unfortunately, a skeptic might suggest that the frequency with which such quotes appear in e-mail signatures indicates a certain deficit of collective imagination.)

Imagination.

Summon it and see that governmental, institutional, and economic levers have become too big and too complicated and too clogged with globalized money to do what needs to be done down here on the ground.

Imagination.

It took one of the greatest acts of collective imagination in history to give birth to the United States of America. Thinking big was what that moment in history required and the result was a new nation and a new democracy. In today's world of global, instantaneous everything and climate change, it will take a new kind of collective imagination to reaffirm the value of the small, the slow, and the local, nurturing a new generation of healthy communities, healthy bioregions, healthy watersheds, healthy foodsheds, and healthy... *moneysheds.*

Imagination.

Of course, poetic flourishes and references to arcs of history are unexpected in a discussion about food and finance. Perhaps even a little off-putting. But here are a few things that are even more off-putting:

—   Hundreds of grams of unaccounted for plutonium in Kazakhstan
—   720 milligrams of salt in an 8-ounce soup can
—   Drone regulations that don't have a prayer
—   Counting on the stock market for an outcome that's fair

I also find brow beating, ideological zeal, righteous indignation, climate change denial, falling water levels in the Colorado River, and the rise of the lowest common denominator not just off-putting, but scary.

So, in response to all of the above, and as inevitably as Left Hand Creek wends its way to St. Vrain Creek on the way to the South Platte, and the letter "J" finds its way between a first name and a last, I now ask:

> *Can we summon the collective imagination*
> *to bring some of our money back down to earth?*

* * * * *

Which leaves unanswered another question, for those who read Part One: *Who is Georgescu-Roegen?*

Nicholas Georgescu-Roegen occupies an important place in the history of economic thought. He was one of the first 20th century economists to posit that economics is ultimately subordinate to the Second Law of Thermodynamics, or, put another way, that the earth's carrying capacity and ecological limits ultimately trump economics. This belief is still considered heretical, or largely irrelevant, by most economists.

Now, before you are deterred from further reading by discussions of economic history, let me reassure you that what we are up to, here, is as earnestly pragmatic as it is irreverently poetic.

What is more pragmatic than increasing the availability of local food? What is more poetic than a beautiful farm-to-table dinner? This is a way for us to put in place a few neighborly pieces of a puzzle that is vexing at the level of economic theory, systems thinking, national policy, or corporate strategy.

There is nothing vexing about a small, diversified, organic farm.

* * * * *

Here's what Georgescu-Roegen said in 1966 in *Analytical Economics*—and note that he was very much a quantitative econometrician, whose work is studded with impenetrable formulas: "For better or worse, we have not yet discovered one single problem of understanding that the Greek philosophers did not formulate."

I'm not suggesting that we have to go all the way back to the ancient Greeks to look for solutions to the loss of jobs in the Rust Belt, the rise of ISIS, or the shelf-life of Twinkies. I *am* suggesting that the arcs of history impel us to reevaluate the roles of technology and finance. Priorities in the 20th century—making global markets stronger, growing cities, industrializing agriculture, computerizing everything, and speeding everything up—need to be revisited in the 21st century. The blur of explosive growth makes it easy to forget that economic progress is not synonymous with health. It is easy to forget even relatively recent arcs of history.

Take, for instance, the arc of history that connects the counterculture of the sixties and seventies to the political dysfunction of today.

In the sixties, we had millions of angry young peaceniks. Today, we have millions of angry displaced factory workers. Hippies rejected the establishment then. Angry voters reject the elite today. It is sobering to think that all the progress of the past 50 years—voting rights, women's rights, gay rights, landing on the moon, biotechnology, smart phones, the first black President, add to this list what you like—delivered us from the hippies only to drop us at the doorstep of today's angry factory workers, with the structural ills of the economy getting worse, all the while.

An increase in the portion of our national budget spent on the military—from 10% in 1960 to 16% today (representing 54% of total discretionary spending and 37% of total world military expenditures)—is a structural ill. An increase in the percentage of corporate profits generated from the financial sector—from 7% in 1960 to around 30% today—accompanying a decrease in the percentage of corporate profits generated from manufacturing—from 50% in 1960 to 25% today—is a structural ill. A decrease in the amount of each American consumer's food dollar that goes to the farmer—from 40 cents in 1900 to 7 cents today—is a structural ill. An increase in health care expenditures—from 5% of GDP in 1960 to 18% in 2016—is a structural ill (particularly in light of our ranking 26th globally in infant mortality and our trajectory towards a third of Americans having diabetes by 2050).

To begin moving in a new direction, we are going to need more than the protests of hippies and the quarrels of angry voters. We're going to need some good old Thoreauvian fiduciary activism.

* * * * *

ENTER: The Stay Puft Marshmallow Man.

Remember the movie *Ghostbusters*? The Ghostbusters were trying to empty their heads of all thoughts, because, courtesy of an evil spell, whatever they thought of next would appear, intent on wreaking havoc. Dan Aykroyd's character, Dr. Ray Stantz, couldn't help himself. Suddenly, a twenty-story-tall, puffy, angry, white, manufactured-food-product monster was lumbering menacingly down a New York

City artery and Stantz could do nothing but ruefully confess, with goofy resignation, what had just popped into his head: "It's the Stay Puft Marshmallow Man."

Which makes me think, at this particular moment, "It's the Thoreauvian Fiduciary Activist." Not marching down the street in a movie, destroying buildings as he goes, but gently sneaking into our hearts and minds, reaching out to us, stirring affection and humility, inviting us to join a conversation that has been going on since the first shekel purchased the first bushel of wheat, and, much later, the first nail was banged into the floor joists of Thoreau's cabin beside Walden Pond.

After the Wall Street occupiers have left Zuccotti Park and the Water Protectors are gone from Standing Rock, after universities and church endowments have divested from fossil fuel, after all the pink-hatted marchers have gone home and the filibusterers have lost steam, after all the high fructose corn syrup has been removed from all the junk food and the last Twinkie has been sequestered in a basement vault at the Museum of Twentieth Century Mouthfeel,[6] Shelf-life, and Cheap Calories, it falls to each of us to get in touch with our inner Thoreauvian fiduciary activist.

* * * * *

Henry David Thoreau lived 200 years ago, but his influence continues, inspiring the likes of Tolstoy, Gandhi, Martin Luther King Jr., E.F. Schumacher, Wendell Berry, and Bill McKibben, to name an illustrious few.

Thoreau's *Walden* set the bar of thinking and doing so poetically high and yet so pragmatically down to earth that it just may be that no one will ever again get over it or under it quite as eloquently and profoundly:

> "Our inventions are wont to be pretty toys, which distract our attention from serious things. They are but improved means to an unimproved end."

> "A man is rich in proportion to the number of things which he can afford to let alone."

> "There are a thousand hacking at the branches of evil to one who is striking at the root, and it may be that he who bestows the largest amount of time and money on the needy is doing the most by his mode of life to produce that misery which he strives in vain to relieve."

6   Mouthfeel is a term used by food technologists to describe a food's physical and chemical interactions in the mouth, which interactions are engineered into food products through the addition of manufactured ingredients and the use of processing techniques. Mouthfeel characteristics include density, dryness, fracturability (including crumbliness, crispiness, and brittleness), graininess, gumminess, hardness, heaviness, moisture absorption (amount of saliva absorbed by product), moisture release, mouthcoating, roughness, slipperiness, smoothness, uniformity, uniformity of bite (evenness of force through bite), uniformity of chew (degree to which the chewing characteristics are even throughout mastication), and viscosity. Here's an example of the mindfeel that is behind the mouthfeel developed by Gum Technology Corporation: "Want to reduce hydrocolloid use, maintain formula system integrity and create a flavor release with great mouthfeel? Gum Technology Corp. suggests processors try the company's Coyote Brand GumPlete stabilizing systems. New GumPlete systems are designed so the starch and gums work synergistically–rather than compete with one another. Processors also can balance cost savings and product improvement with Hydro-Fi, a new generation of texturizers. A unique combination of Coyote brand hydrocolloids and Citri-Fi citrus fiber, Hydro-Fi improves texture and yield and enhances mouthfeel." (Gum Technology Corporation website)

In an article titled "Managing the Mouthfeel of Dairy Products," Donna Berry reviews texturants developed by a number of companies, including Solazyme, Penfield Food Ingredients, Agropur Ingredients, and Glanbia Nutritionals: "With most dairy products, formulators are challenged with preventing protein aggregation, gritty or chalky mouthfeel, thinness, settling of insoluble ingredients, and visual separation. Texturants can assist with stabilization, suspension, and thickening. They make it possible to produce consumer-appealing dairy foods with a consistent, uniform quality." (*Food Business News*, July 15, 2014)

We are still figuring out, today, the relationship between means and ends, between economy and culture. The dissonance between how we make money and whether it is possible to give back enough to redress the ills inherent in the way we made that money is, still, the crux of the matter.

The modern economy has created 2,043 billionaires with a combined net worth of almost $8 trillion (up 18% in 2016); the wealthiest 1% of the world's population owns more than everyone else combined; almost three billion people around the world have come to own smart phones in a little more than a decade; 86,000 private foundations in the U.S. have over $700 billion in assets; and yet this very same momentum of wealth creation and consumerism prevents us from responding adequately to the most fundamental crises of our time.

Thoreau's wildly prescient words in *Civil Disobedience* still ring true for anyone concerned about how, despite best intentions, our money finds its way to distant activities in which we do not believe:

> I do not care to trace the course of my dollar, if I could, till it buys a man or a musket to shoot one with—the dollar is innocent—but I am concerned to trace the effects of my allegiance [...]

> I quarrel not with far-off foes, but with those who, near at home, cooperate with, and do the bidding of, those far away, and without whom the latter would be harmless [...]

> It is truly enough said that a corporation has no conscience; but a corporation of conscientious men is a corporation *with* a conscience. Law never made men a whit more just; and, by means of their respect for it, even the well-disposed are daily made the agents of injustice. A common and natural result of an undue respect for law is, that you may see a file of soldiers, colonel, captain, corporal, privates, powder-monkeys, and all, marching in admirable order over hill and dale to wars, against their wills, ay, against their common sense and consciences, which makes it very steep marching indeed, and produces a palpitation of the heart. They have no doubt that it is a damnable business in which they are concerned; they are all peaceably inclined.

Where Thoreau refers to law, I hear markets. (Reread the preceding paragraph making that substitution.)

So, I believe that the most conscientious thing I can do is bring some of my money closer to home, shortening the distance between me and that which my money supports, lessening my complicity in distant ills and increasing my connection to things that I can support directly.

* * * * *

In times of war, we've always had conscientious objectors. In times of economic and political befuddlement, can we encourage a corps of *conscientious investors?* It's a bit risky bringing up conscientious objecting, here, as it suggests that only peaceniks should mobilize to invest in local food systems. I'm taking the risk of that confusion because there is something in the concept of conscientious investing that is worth reflecting upon.

Objecting and protesting are, of course, cornerstones of democracy. Perhaps we need to rethink investing in a similar light. We tend to see investing as something to be done in private, looking inward, all about personal gain. We tend not to see it as a way of protesting or supporting, but, rather, purely as a numbers game. What if we looked at investing the same way we look at protesting? As a cornerstone of democracy? As a way for us to take a stand? As a way for us to connect with others around shared concerns, looking outward, focusing on societal health?

Now, I'm not talking about turning the entire conventional idea of investing on its head. (Kind of like turning the word SOIL on its head... but I get ahead of myself. More on that later.) Or, should we say, I *am* talking about turning the idea of investing on its head—but only for a few minutes a day, so that blood can flow in a different direction.

* * * * *

"We need economists and climatologists and marine biologists and hydrologists and politicians and geologists and industrialists and environmentalists all at the same table," said a speaker at a recent renewable energy conference. "We need to think in terms of whole systems. We need multi-sectoral, interdisciplinary solutions."

While she spoke, I thought of conference upon conference, report upon report, scientific study upon economic model, flow chart upon org chart, yards of elaborate graphic facilitations taped up on workshop walls, feedback loop upon feedback loop, certification upon certification, corporate disclosure upon corporate disclosure, policy upon policy, regulation upon regulation.

And then I thought about making a loan to a local organic farmer.

* * * * *

Imagination.

If we summon enough of it, can we see beyond multisyllabic economic and agricultural and technical jargon: sustainable, restorative, regenerative... wait... isn't it just healthy that we're after? As in, a *healthy* economy? As in, Agriculture for a Healthy America? Or is it Americans for Healthy Agriculture? AHA. *AHA!*

Imagination.

I've always been struck by one of Thoreau's more convoluted sentences, "How can he remember well his ignorance, which his growth requires, who has so often to use his knowledge?"

How can we reckon well our whereabouts, which *AHA!* moments require, who have so often to use our financial knowledge?

II   Return

Salmon return. Boomerangs return. Hindus return. When things work out, investments return. Letters with insufficient postage return. So do infections, mosquitos, prodigal sons, wandering eyes, sideways glances, the hands of a clock, circular reasons, not-quite-infinite seasons, pendulums, memories, criminals to the scenes of their crimes, and stories to where they left off. Prior to the advent of Colony Collapse Disorder, bees returned. Heroes, real and mythic, return: Odysseus, Columbus, General Douglas MacArthur. Too many winks, verdicts, and tennis serves have been returned over the course of human history to be counted. The same goes for sweaters after Christmas. And, as long as there have been neighbors, economists, democratic entanglements, and governments, there have been many happy returns, diminishing returns, election returns, and tax returns.

Through it all, however, through all these physical, spiritual, emotional, postal, historical, mythical, electoral, recreational, and commercial goings and comings, there is one thing, in our infinite, industrial wisdom and pioneering spirit, that we haven't returned.

Carbon.

* * * * *

Lulled into frenzied complacency by internal combustion and industrialization, we've taken carbon from the earth and put it into the atmosphere, treating an elegant, billions-of-years-in-the-making system of solar energy, cellular biology, photosynthesis, and carbon cycling as if it were a one-way street. The end result? An economy of tailpipes, smokestacks, superstores, turbo-charged financial markets, and petrochemical-doused industrial agriculture.

And the Mother of All End Results, climate change.

And the Sisters of All End Results, distrust and befuddlement.

Paul Newman, Sir Albert Howard, and armies of soil critters to the rescue.

* * * * *

Even in the era of venture capital Moonshots and billion-dollar Mars-shots, re-turning is as important as venturing forth. Coming back down to earth. Returning to "the ignorance which our growth requires." Returning to humility and civility.

It wasn't just a cute turn of phrase when Thomas Jefferson said, "Cultivators of the earth are the most valuable citizens." Or when FDR said, "A nation that destroys its soil destroys itself." Or when Paul Newman said, "In life, we should be a little like the farmer, who puts back into the soil what he takes out." Or when the founder of the Earthworm School of Fiduciary Responsibility and Peaceable Finance conjures up the Thoreauvian Fiduciary Activist.

But, not to worry, you won't find the words Thoreauvian, fiduciary, or activism on a bottle of Newman's Own salad dressing. Or in any Presidential proclamations. Or in an investment prospectus. For that matter, you may never see them again in a discussion of Slow Money or something called SOIL—Slow Opportunities for Investing Locally. Because they are awfully complicated terms for something as simple as making 0% loans to local farmers and food entrepreneurs.

* * * * *

We live in a world in which the complicated has been made simple and the simple has been made complicated.

Pushing the power button on your computer, simple. Having an authentic con-versation with your neighbor, complicated. Buying a bag of potato chips, simple. Growing potatoes in your front yard, complicated. Owning a diversified portfolio of gold stocks, simple. Making a loan to a farmer down the road, complicated.

So, forget about matters of the Thoreauvian or fiduciary kind and think about the farmer down the road. And about Newman's Own.

* * * * *

How beautifully simple. Giving away all the profits:

> Our "100% of Profits to Charity" commitment is one of two founding values upon which Newman's Own is built (the other being "Quality Will Always Trump the Bottom Line"). It's a very important part of our story, it's in our DNA, it's why we exist, it motivates all of us, and it's the true heart of Newman's Own. We are proud of this commitment, and, especially in these times of so many promotional programs tying business sales to social purpose, want to be

clear and unambiguous about what we mean when we say "100% of Profits to Charity." It's not something we just thought up to boost sales, it's not a play on words, and one shouldn't need an accounting degree to understand it. We have been doing it for close to 35 years, and as of May 2017, have donated over $490 million to thousands of deserving organizations around the world.[1]

1   http://www.newmansown.com/
     100-percent-profits-to-charity/

How beautifully worth repeating, Paul Newman's words, "In life, we should be a little like the farmer, who puts back into the soil what he takes out."

How beautifully fundamental, rejiggering the ethos of business, splicing altruism into entrepreneurship and consumerism in ways no one had ever imagined.

What made Newman's Own possible was, of course, Newman. Which is not to say that you have to be an impossibly charismatic celebrity to be altruistic. Only, that you have to be an authentic individual. You need to muster the gumption to tune out the experts, the professional permission givers and takers, the intermediaries and the naysayers, and find ways to act authentically.

For some, authenticity means competing for market share. For others, authenticity means terroir.[2] For some, authenticity means protesting. For others, it means leaving a field fallow. For some, it means paying taxes. For others, avoiding them. For some, belonging to a church. For others, belonging to a CSA. For some, hot dogs. For others, organic apple pie. For some, ethanol. For others, earthworms. For some, conscientious objecting. For others, conscientious investing. For some, giving away 1% of revenue. For others, giving away all the profits.

2   The soil and microclimate that give
     a food its particular taste.

* * * * *

Sir Albert Howard's Law of Return is, it seems to me, as authentic as it gets.

Howard wrote *An Agricultural Testament* and *The Soil and Health* in the mid-twentieth century, based on his observation of soil building practices in India, where he was a government scientist. His concepts of farming in concert with nature show the way, still, for many of the *AHA!* persuasion. Here is a little of Sir Albert Howard's vision, as digested by poet farmer Wendell Berry:

> The balance between growth and decay is the sole principle of stability in nature and in agriculture. And this balance is never static, never fully achieved, for it is dependent upon a cycle, which in nature, and within the limits of nature, is self-sustaining, but which in agriculture must be made continuous by purpose

and by correct methods. "This cycle," Howard wrote, "is constituted of the successive and repeated processes of birth, growth, maturity, death, and decay."

The interaction, the interdependence, of life and death, which in nature is the source of an inexhaustible fecundity, is the basis of a set of analogies, to which agriculture and the rest of the human economy must conform in order to endure, and which is ultimately religious, as Howard knew, "An eastern religion calls this cycle the Wheel of Life [...] Death supersedes life and life rises again from what is dead and decayed."

The maintenance of this cycle is the practical basis of good farming and its moral basis as well:

> The correct relation between the processes of growth and the processes of decay is the first principle of successful farming. Agriculture must always be balanced. If we speed up growth we must accelerate decay. If, on the other hand, the soil's reserves are squandered, crop production ceases to be good farming; it becomes something very different. The farmer is transformed into a bandit.[3]

3   *The Soil and Health*, Sir Albert Howard, Introduction by Wendell Berry (University Press of Kentucky, 2006) p. xvii

What Howard called banditry is referred to by many of today's proponents of healthy agriculture as mining. We are mining soil fertility. In order to maximize efficiency, we apply industrial practices to farming, turning farms into factories and focusing on productivity rather than fertility. Over time, life in the soil is degraded. And, it turns out, so is the health of communities and the health of democracy.

In recent years, the degradation of community and the dysfunction of democratic institutions have become impossible to ignore; what is far easier to overlook, but no less important, and integral to many related processes of cultural and ecological decline, is the degradation of the soil.

* * * * *

Based on competing worldviews and the related interpretation of data, it may be possible for two equally patriotic individuals to disagree about the meaning of the decline of the family farm and the consolidation of the agricultural sector in large, industrial farms. Or about the significance of the decline during the 20th century in the number of plant varieties in commercial cultivation. Or about the tillage of hundreds of millions of acres and the application of hundreds of millions of tons of synthetic fertilizer, herbicides, and pesticides. Or about the vulnerability of increasingly long and complex supply chains in the food system. Or about the role of ruminants and manure. Or about the safety of GMOs and raw milk.

The room for disagreement between these same two individuals is far smaller, I'd like to imagine, when it comes to the following proposition:

SOIL TEEMING WITH LIFE, GOOD; LIFELESS SOIL, BAD.

Just how good the good is and how bad the bad is... well, that, as Shakespeare sort of put it, is the question.

* * * * *

While I was searching for images of life in the soil, I came upon the following on Sweet Bay Farm's website (see margin). They're working to restore soils depleted by decades of monoculture—the continual cultivation of a single crop, in this case tobacco—so this picture of several earthworm tunnels in a clod does not yet suggest anything teeming. Charles Darwin's observation, in his last manuscript, is instructive with respect to the magnitude of earthworm populations in general:

Soil sample from Sweet Bay Farm, showing earthworm tunnels and fungi threads. *(https://farmingsweetbay. wordpress.com/)*

> Hensen, who has published so full and interesting an account of the habits of worms, calculates, from the number which he found in a measured space, that there must exist 133,000 living worms in a hectare of land, or 53,767 in an acre. This latter number of worms would weigh 356 pounds, taking Hensen's standard of the weight of a single worm, namely three grams. It should, however, be noted that this calculation is founded on the numbers found in a garden, and Hensen believes that worms are here twice as numerous as in cornfields. The above results, astonishing though they be, seem to me credible, judging from the number of worms which I have sometimes seen.[4]

But Darwin's numbers were only the beginning. In 1951 (the year this author joined the ranks of the Baby Boomers), observers of pastureland in Scotland estimated the number of earthworms per acre to be 100,000 to 200,000. Today, the United States Department of Agriculture Natural Resources Conservation Service (NRCS) reports that the number of earthworms per acre of cropland can exceed a million, if the land is "highly organic."[5]

4   *The Formation of Vegetable Mould Through the Action of Worms, With Observations on Their Habits*, Charles Darwin (John Murray, 1881 and Faber and Faber, 1966) p. 84

5   See a dramatic comparison of earthworm populations in organic vs. conventional farmland in Boone County, Iowa, in the National Research Council's *Toward Sustainable Agricultural Systems in the 21st Century* (The National Academies Press, 2010) p. 382

The NRCS cites the following beneficial soil fertility services performed by earthworms:

Stimulate microbial activity. Although earthworms derive their nutrition from microorganisms, many more microorganisms are present in their feces or casts than in the organic matter that they consume. As organic matter passes through their intestines, it is fragmented and inoculated with microorganisms. Increased microbial activity facilitates the cycling of nutrients from organic matter and their conversion into forms readily taken up by plants.

Mix and aggregate soil. As they consume organic matter and mineral particles, earthworms excrete wastes in the form of casts, a type of soil aggregate. Charles Darwin calculated that earthworms can move large amounts of soil from the lower strata to the surface and also carry organic matter down into deeper soil layers. A large proportion of soil passes through the guts of earthworms, and they can turn over the top six inches (15 cm) of soil in ten to twenty years.

Increase infiltration. Earthworms enhance porosity as they move through the soil. Some species make permanent burrows deep into the soil. These burrows can persist long after the inhabitant has died, and can be a major conduit for soil drainage, particularly under heavy rainfall. At the same time, the burrows minimize surface water erosion. The horizontal burrowing of other species in the top several inches of soil increases overall porosity and drainage.

Improve water-holding capacity. By fragmenting organic matter, and increasing soil porosity and aggregation, earthworms can significantly increase the water-holding capacity of soils.

Provide channels for root growth. The channels made by deep-burrowing earthworms are lined with readily available nutrients and make it easier for roots to penetrate deep into the soil.

Bury and shred plant residue. Plant and crop residue are gradually buried by cast material deposited on the surface and as earthworms pull surface residue into their burrows.

Earthworms are joined in the soil by many other invertebrates, including millipedes, centipedes, springtails, grubs, beetles, and snails. But the first point in the above list of earthworm functions, referring to the stimulation of microbial activity, is our conceptual wormhole to a whole other realm—the realm of myriad soil creatures that we cannot see with the naked eye.[6] This is, truly, the realm of teeming. Bacteria,

6   According to *Popular Science*, "A wormhole is [...] deformed space that has warped in such a way as to connect two different points in space-time. The result is a tunnel-like structure that could be straight or curved, linking two areas of the Universe that are incredibly far apart. Einsteinian mathematical models predict that wormholes exist, but none have ever been found."

fungi, protozoa, nematodes, mites, microarthropods—there can be 10,000 to 50,000 species in less than a teaspoon of soil. That's *species*. In terms of individuals, there are more microbes in a teaspoon of soil than there are humans on earth. Bacteria, actinomycetes, and fungi in an acre of soil can weigh thousands of pounds. Some estimates suggest that microbes account for half the weight of all life on earth.[7]

David Suzuki's *The Sacred Balance* offers the following:

RELATIVE NUMBER OF SOIL FLORA AND FAUNA IN SURFACE SOIL

ORGANISMS	NUMBER/METRE^2	NUMBER/GRAM
MICROFLORA		
Bacteria	10^{13}–10^{14}	10^8–10^9
Actinomycetes	10^{12}–10^{13}	10^7–10^8
Fungi	10^{10}–10^{11}	10^5–10^6
Algae	10^9–10^{10}	10^4–10^5
MICROFAUNA		
Protozoa	10^9–10^{10}	10^4–10^5
Nematoda	10^6–10^7	10–10^2
Other Fauna	10^3–10^5	

Microorganisms also live in the guts of earthworms—500,000 or so per worm.[8] They are found in more astonishing numbers in the guts of humans. Recent studies indicate that 1,000 species and tens of trillions of microbes live in the human digestive tract, with as many as 100 trillion in total occupying each human body. Multiply this by the global human population of 7 billion or so and you arrive at an astounding 700,000,000,000,000,000,000,000,000, if I have the zeroes right, which I may not. Is that 700 septillion? Such a name seems far too reductionist for the enormity it denotes.

* * * * *

The names of big numbers don't do justice to our understanding of the underlying nature of things. Take trillions, for example. We talk of wars costing trillions of dollars and the U.S. gross domestic product of $18 trillion and world economic output of $75 trillion and $250 trillion of total global financial assets and trillions of dollars a day flowing through currency markets. But do we really know what

7   *The Hidden Half of Nature: The Microbial Roots of Life and Health*, David Montgomery and Ann Biklé (Norton & Co., 2016) p. 25. Also see the work of David Zuberer at Texas A&M University.

8   *Biology of Earthworms*, Edwards and Lofty (Chapman and Hall, London, 1972) p. 156. While Denis Hayes was organizing the first Earth Day in 1970, C.A. Edwards and J.R. Lofty (the latter an intriguing name for one focused on matters of the subterranean kind) were gathering data for their book, still one of the definitive texts on this subject.

the number one trillion means? Do we have any frame of reference that can give this number a context to which we can relate?

I know I didn't until my encounter with Jerome McGeorge, friend and financial advisor to George Siemon and Theresa Marquez, leaders of CROPP, the $1 billion farmer-owned cooperative behind the leading organic food brand Organic Valley.

"I want to see what Jerome thinks of Slow Money," George said to me, as we drove up to a rustic home outside La Farge, Wisconsin.

Here's how one journalist describes Jerome:

> Jerome McGeorge, a 70-year-old man with long white hair and a wispy beard, is the wizard I'm looking for. He was a founding member of Coulee Region Organic Produce Pool (CROPP), the cooperative that owns the Organic Valley brand, and an old hippy straight out of the Summer of Love. One moment he is describing the revolutionary spirit of late 1960s San Francisco, the next he's on to peak food, the price of organic milk in Europe, mission versus profit motivated enterprises, and the long, slow death of the family farm during his lifetime.[9]

I've long forgotten what I said to Jerome during that visit, perhaps because I was taken aback by his soothsayerly demeanor. Was I to take him seriously? Was he to take me seriously? Would he dismiss my explanations of fast money and slow money as mumbo jumbo? His reception proved far too warm for any such anxiety to linger.

"Here's something that you need to know," Jerome said to me. "I'm going to start you off with a fact, and then ask you two questions. The fact is, A million seconds equals 12 days. The first question is, How long is a billion seconds?"

I don't remember if I came up with the correct answer: 12,000 days, otherwise known as 32.9 years.

"Now, here's the second question," Jerome continued, "How long is a trillion seconds?"

Again, I don't remember if I came up with the correct answer: 32,900 years.

A million seconds equals 12 days and a trillion seconds equals 32,900 years. That's how much bigger a trillion is than a million.

9   Sascha Matuszak, in a blog titled *The Driftless Manifesto*. (http://roadsandkingdoms.com/2015/the-driftless-manifesto/)

Expressing the quantity one trillion as time instead of as an imaginary stack of dollar bills makes it somewhat more comprehensible. For instance, a stack of one trillion dollar bills would be 67,866 miles high, reaching a quarter of the way to the moon. This is remarkable, to be sure, but it doesn't quite tickle my imagination the way this does: If someone had lent Jesus $1 trillion at zero percent interest on the day he was born, and it was to be paid back by him and those who came after at the rate of $1 million per day, payments would still have more than 500 years to go.

I'd worked in a small venture capital fund in New York City in the 1980s and as treasurer of a $60 million foundation in the 1990s and with a national network of sustainability-minded angel investors for another decade, reviewing who knows how many business plans with financial projections showing hundreds of millions of dollars or more of sales within five years, but until that day in Jerome's living room decades later, I didn't have an authentic feel, a wizard-enhanced feel, for the implications of billions and trillions.

In terms of money and the flow of capital through complex securities, millisecond computer trades, and financial institutions that are Too Big To Fail, trillions means *mind-numbing*.

In terms of microbes and life in the soil, trillions means *teeming*.

* * * * *

From Jerome to Jeremy.

"Hi, I'm Jeremy Grantham." I was taken aback. This was the Bioneers East event, catering to environmental and social activists. Jeremy Grantham is one of the world's top investment managers. Grantham, Mayo, Van Otterloo & Co. has some $80 billion under management and Jeremy's newsletter is widely respected in financial circles.

"You are?" I responded.

"Yes," he said.

"I had no idea there was a real financier in the audience," I quipped, silently replaying the remarks I had just made from the podium about his newsletter and the cover story it had elicited in *The Economist*.

"My daughter-in-law volunteers for Bioneers," he said.

"Am I in trouble?" I asked, half seriously.

"No," he said. "I agreed with most of what you said."

During my public remarks, I'd shown the covers of *TIME* and *The Economist* from the summer of 2009.

TIME displayed a hamburger package, whose label read, "This hamburger may be hazardous to your health. Why the American food system is bad for our bodies, our economy and our environment—and what some visionaries are trying to do about it."

The *TIME* story began:

> Somewhere in Iowa, a pig is being raised in a confined pen, packed in so tightly with other swine that their curly tails have been chopped off so they won't bite one another. To prevent him from getting sick in such close quarters, he is dosed with antibiotics. The waste produced by the pig and his thousands of pen mates on the factory farm where they live goes into manure lagoons that blanket neighboring communities with air pollution and a stomach-churning stench. He's fed on American corn that was grown with the help of government subsidies and millions of tons of chemical fertilizer. When the pig is slaughtered, at about five months of age, he'll become sausage or bacon that will sell cheap, feeding an American addiction to meat that has contributed to an obesity epidemic currently afflicting more than two-thirds of the population. And when the rains come, the excess fertilizer that coaxed so much corn from the ground will be washed into the Mississippi River and down into the Gulf of Mexico, where it will help kill fish for miles and miles around. That's the state of your bacon—circa 2009.

> Horror stories about the food industry have long been with us—ever since 1906, when Upton Sinclair's landmark novel *The Jungle* told some ugly truths about how America produces its meat. In the century that followed, things got much better, and in some ways much worse. The U.S. agricultural industry can now produce unlimited quantities of meat and grains at remarkably cheap prices. But it does so at a high cost to the environment, animals, and humans. Those hidden prices are the creeping erosion of our fertile farmland, cages for egg-laying chickens so packed that the birds can't even raise their wings and the scary rise of antibiotic-resistant bacteria among farm animals. Add to the price tag the acceleration of global warming—our energy-intensive food system uses 19% of U.S. fossil fuels, more than any other sector of the economy.

Then I'd flipped, during my public remarks, to the cover of *The Economist*, observing that structural problems of the industrial food system mirror structural problems of the industrial financial system. Hogs packed into confinement units are a reflection of dollars concentrated in financial instruments and institutions.

This issue of the *The Economist* featured several stories, triggered by Grantham's Quarterly Letter, which called out the efficient market hypothesis, one of the pillars of modern investment theory. Grantham argued that the "desire for mathematical order and elegant models" impelled the "economic establishment" to believe in the efficient market hypothesis, even though it no longer explained market and investor behavior: "The incredibly inaccurate efficient market theory was believed in totality by many of our financial leaders, and believed in part by almost all. It left our economic and government establishment sitting by confidently, even as a lethally dangerous combination of asset bubbles, lax controls, pernicious incentives and wickedly complicated instruments led to our current plight."[10]

"Do you ever get into discussions about Malthus?" Jeremy asked me.

"I try to avoid it," I replied, "because the next thing you know, you're called a Luddite."

"Malthus was right," Jeremy said. "He just had the arithmetic wrong."

For me, this conversation was the next best thing to talking to the Wizard of Oz. Actually, better. Jeremy is the only international money manager of his ilk who is out front on agriculture and limits to growth. This was one of only two instances in over 30 years that I can remember Thomas Malthus' name being mentioned in a business context without derision. The other was a *Wall Street Journal* article on March 24, 2008, titled "New Limits to Growth Revive Malthusian Fears"—eliciting, we can surmise, one of the largest collective eye rolls in that newspaper's history; Malthus is, in the canons of capitalism, the thinker everyone loves to hate.

Around the time America and Adam Smith's "invisible hand" were being born, Malthus was predicting that global population, destined to grow exponentially, would soon outstrip food supplies, destined to grow arithmetically. While his arithmetic, and, therefore, his sense of the immediate future were proven wrong, his basic insight—that economic growth and rising levels of consumption would eventually collide with natural systems—was way ahead of its time, as the *Wall Street Journal* article affirmed:

Where it went wrong—and how the crisis is changing it

10   As reported by Joe Nocera in the *New York Times*, June 5, 2009.

Thomas Malthus

"The power of population is so superior to the power of Earth to produce subsistence for man, that premature death must in some shape or other visit the human race."
- *Thomas Malthus, 1798*

"If the present growth trends in world population, industrialization, pollution, food production, and resource depletion continue unchanged, the limits to growth on this planet will be reached sometime within the next 100 years."
- *The Club of Rome, 1972*

In the past, economic forces spurred solutions. Scarcity of resources led to higher prices, and higher prices eventually led to conservation and innovation. Whale oil was a popular source of lighting in the 19th century. Prices soared in the middle of the century, and people sought other ways to fuel lamps. In 1846, Abraham Gesner began developing kerosene, a cleaner-burning alternative. By the end of the century, whale oil cost less than it did in 1831.

A similar pattern could unfold again. But economic forces alone may not be able to fix the problems this time around. Societies as different as the U.S. and China face stiff political resistance to boosting water prices to encourage efficient use, particularly from farmers. When resources such as water are shared across borders, establishing a pricing framework can be thorny. And in many developing nations, food-subsidy programs make it less likely that rising prices will spur change.

This troubles some economists who used to be skeptical of the premise of "The Limits to Growth." As a young economist 30 years ago, Joseph Stiglitz said flatly, "There is not a persuasive case to be made that we face a problem from the exhaustion of our resources in the short or medium run."

Today, the Nobel laureate is concerned that oil is underpriced relative to the cost of carbon emissions, and that key resources such as water are often provided free. "In the absence of market signals, there's no way the market will solve these problems," he says. "How do we make people who have gotten something for free start paying for it? That's really hard. If our patterns of living, our patterns of consumption are imitated, as others are striving to do, the world probably is not viable."

To the side of the Bioneers stage, my conversation with Jeremy continued, the subject turning to the power of compound growth. He offered the following quiz:

Q: Assume the personal possessions of an ancient Egyptian were all squeezed together into one square cubic yard. If that cubic yard expanded by 4.5% compounded annually, how big would it be today?

A: Nine trillion times bigger. That's a billion times bigger than our solar system.

* * * * *

Compound growth sneaks up on you. So does ever-accelerating change.

The astounding pace of change that has characterized recent decades has its roots in what Gordon Moore, one of the founders of Intel, foresaw in 1968. Moore's Law, as it came to be known, predicted that computer power would grow exponentially, doubling every two years or so. Astonishingly, it has done this for the ensuing 50 years. Here's how Intel CEO Brian Krzanich explains it:

> If you took Intel's first-generation microchip from 1971, the 4004, and the latest chip Intel has on the market today, the sixth-generation Intel Core processor, you will see that Intel's latest chip offers 3,500 times more performance, is 90,000 times more energy efficient, and is about 60,000 times lower in cost. To put it more vividly, Intel engineers did a rough calculation of what would happen had a 1971 Volkswagen Beetle improved at the same rate as microchips did under Moore's Law. These are the numbers: Today, that Beetle would be able to go about three hundred thousand miles per hour. It would get two million miles per gallon of gas, and it would cost four cents![11]

Around the same time that Moore was formulating his law, Alvin Toffler was writing *Future Shock*, a best-selling shot across the bow with respect to the social disorientation which we had in store: "The acceleration of change does not merely buffet industries or nations. It is a concrete force that reaches deep into our personal lives, compels us to act out new roles, and confronts us with the danger of a new and powerfully upsetting psychological disease. This new disease can be called 'future shock.'"[12]

Some of the statistics Toffler used seem almost quaint, today, as they track such trends as the acceleration of transportation and the transmission of knowledge (mostly, up to that point, via publishing) from the dawn of civilization up to 1970, missing the hyper-acceleration that was only then beginning. For instance, it took the human race all of recorded history up to the end of the 19th century to break 100 MPH, courtesy of the steam locomotive; then, it took only 58 years for airplanes to reach 400 MPH; then, it took only 25 years to double that speed record again; and, by the end of the 1960s, men were orbiting the earth at 18,000 MPH.

Even before Moore's law could manifest itself in a realm that rippled through so many others, and prior to the shortest doubling period ever for human population—from 3 billion in 1960 to 6 billion in 1999—Toffler concluded, "The pattern, here and in a thousand other statistical series, is absolutely clear and unmistakable. Millennia or centuries go by, and then, in our own times, a sudden bursting of the limits, a fantastic spurt forward. The reason for this is that technology feeds on itself."

11 *Thank You for Being Late: An Optimist's Guide to Thriving in the Age of Accelerations*, Thomas Friedman (Farrar, Straus and Giroux, 2016) p. 36

12 *Future Shock*, Alvin Toffler (Random House, 1970) p. 12

Today, Robert Colvile calls it The Great Acceleration and Thomas Friedman calls it the Age of Accelerations, referring to three simultaneous trajectories of exponential growth in technology, globalization, and climate change:

> We have no choice but to adapt to this new pace of change. It will be harder and require more self-motivation—and that reality is surely one of the things roiling politics all over the world today, particularly in America and Europe. The accelerations we've charted have indeed opened a wide gap between the pace of technological change, globalization, and environmental stresses and the ability of people and governing systems to adapt to and manage them.[13]

Listening to this sense of inevitability, echoed by so many, it does seem that we live not only in the Age of Accelerations, but also in the Binary Age, the Age of Ones and Zeros, the age that seems so full of its own prowess that it is all too ready to choose the Technological Either over the Malthusian Or:

> Acceleration is so baked into the system that [...] even if the West were to retreat from haste and hustle, it is too late—the virus has escaped from its laboratory and infected the rest of the world with a desire to consume, innovate, and disrupt [...]

> Yes, the relentless machinery of acceleration has caused many of our ecological problems—but it also offers us the tools to outgrow and out-think them. We just have to use those tools wisely [...]

> The nature of 21st century society, its most basic setting, is to accelerate—which is why speed is, and will remain, the most important force in our lives. This process will inevitably bring terrors as well as wonder: The price of a faster pace is a bumpier ride. Yet on balance, an accelerated future is one we will surely rush to embrace.[14]

* * * * *

We should not be surprised that this culture of speed would create the conditions within which a countercultural movement reaffirming "slow" would emerge. Slow Food, Slow Cities, Slow Money, and other grassroots networks offer alternatives to faster, bigger, more global. Picking up where E.F. Schumacher's *Small Is Beautiful* left off, these groups promote "slow" as a matter of counterbalance, precaution, diversity, personal and societal health, community resilience, aesthetics, and ethics.

13   Friedman, p. 198

14   *The Great Acceleration: How the World Is Getting Faster, Faster,* Robert Colvile (Bloomsbury, 2016) pp. 312–326

Describing Terra Madre, an international network of food communities, Slow Food founder Carlo Petrini states:

> Food is politics, respect for diversity is politics, the way in which we care for nature is politics—Terra Madre is politics. There is nothing belittling about the fact that this kind of politics is poetically nuanced, that here the beautiful and the noble fuse with the serious and the tangible. Ethics and aesthetics can no longer be kept separate. The poetry and politics of Terra Madre teach the world to stop brutalizing itself, to halt the process of global homogenization that is debasing people and depriving them of any power of self-determination.[15]

15   *Terra Madre: Forging a New Global Network of Sustainable Food Communities,* Carlo Petrini (Chelsea Green, 2009) p. 14

Slow Food connects food communities around the world in what Petrini calls "virtuous globalization," defending cultural alternatives to fast food, resisting the excesses of industrial efficiency and consumerism, celebrating biological and cultural diversity, and countering "the insidious virus" of speed.

The need for interludes of slowness in an increasingly harried world could not be more obvious. But is this just an occasional tonic for a few? Or does it signal more widespread cultural transformation to come?

In an article called "The Great Deceleration," Alex Jensen addresses issues of economic growth and acceleration head on. Citing a plethora of daunting statistics about the 20-fold growth of the global economy in the 20th century, with an accompanying growth in demand for natural resources of between 600 and 2,000 percent, he writes:

> The increasing scale of economic activity, of "the economy," is the heart of the multiple interlocking crises that beset societies and the earth today. The relentlessly expansionist logic of the system is inimical to life, to the world, even to genuine well-being; so, if we wish to instead honor, defend, and respect life and the world, we must upend that logic, and begin the urgent task of downscaling economic activity and the system that drives it, the "Great Deceleration."

Nevertheless, from every organ of the establishment, where the commercial mind reigns, we hear that the challenge before us is not deceleration, but making the acceleration even greater, of stepping harder on the gas pedal, of ramping up production and consumption (and, thus, waste and pollution). Even as governments expound solemnly on the need to arrest climate change and promote Sustainable Development Goals on the one hand, they are on the other handing over nearly boundless subsidies to industry, pushing for the expansion of global trade, and otherwise facilitating the acceleration of acceleration.

After such a daunting peek at the most fundamental of macroeconomic and ecological matters, and wondering whether the emperor of economics has no clothes, and wondering, too, whether the most powerful "organ of the establishment" isn't right here between my own ears, there's nothing like a little slow food to calm the nerves.

So: *Here's to Sardinian pecorino, Smilyan beans, Ragya yak cheese, Canapu cowpeas, Ococuri potatoes, Organic Valley Grassmilk, Dehradun basmati, Castello di Verduno Nebbiolo, Golden Coast Mead, Red Wagon Farm radishes, St. Benoit Yogurt, Mountain Flower goat milk, Western Daughters grassfed ground beef, Cornish Salt pilchards, Tehuacán Valley amaranth, Pardailhan Black Turnips, Guinea-Bissau cashews, Mirandesa sausage, White Oak Pasture bone broth, McCauley Family Farm Pickled Beets, the folks at Colorful Ranch and Zephyros Farm and Ollin Farms and Native Hill Farm and 63rd Street Farm and Black Cat and Golden Hoof and Aspen Moon and Sustainable Settings and Cure Organic Farm, Babettes' Barley-Flake Porridge bread, Morton's peaches, and Don Studinski's Slow Honey!*

* * * * *

Back at our impromptu *tête-à-tête* by the Bioneers stage, as Jeremy Grantham and I were winding up, I asked, buoyed by the many items on which we had so readily agreed, "Do you think we can get a million investors to invest 1% of their money in local food systems?"

"No," Jeremy responded flatly. "It's too much of a leap for most folks."

"What if I could convince you," I retorted, "that there's a 1% chance that if you gave Slow Money 1% of your foundation's assets, we could get a million people to follow you?"

"I like your arithmetic," Jeremy replied, with a smile.

This is the arithmetic of speed and scale. Tiny fractions of humongous pools of capital act on the number-craving mind like pheromones. This is also the physics of trim tabs, a metaphor often used by those seeking to change large institutions and entrenched systems. Small adjustments in trim tabs change the direction of the largest supertankers.

Arithmetic and physics notwithstanding, there was Jeremy Grantham's smile. I'll take it. Happily. In fact, I extend an invitation to you, friends from this side and that of the Continental Divide, and perhaps, too, from this side and that of other divides, as well. This is an invitation to appreciate that smile.

There was a lot in it. A pinch of respect for entrepreneurial zeal. A recognition of long odds. A reverence for the power of markets. A preference for large numbers. A dash of Twainish "The only problem with tainted money is t'aint enough of it." An intimation of conundrums wrapped in enigmas that sprout like dandelions in the no man's land between investing and philanthropy. A realization that modern finance is a lens through which you can peer into distant fiduciary galaxies, seeking to discover far-flung opportunities to hedge risk, but turn that lens towards the ground beneath your feet and... well...

* * * * *

You certainly won't see what David Montgomery and Ann Biklé saw when they zeroed in on the microbes in their garden and in their own digestive tracts:

The root is the gut and the gut is the root!

It's probably not a coincidence that the majority of the bacteria in the gut and in the soil share a saprophyte genealogy (from Greek, sapro refers to rotting things and phyte means "plant"). In both places, the bacteria that are present specialize in decomposing plant matter.

If you were to turn a plant root inside out, rhizosphere and all, you would see that it is like the digestive tract. The two are, in many respects, parallel universes. The biology and processes that bind soil, roots, and rhizosphere together mirror those in the mucosal lining of the gut and the associated immune tissue. The gut is the human version of the rhizosphere, the part of our bodies incredibly rich with specially recruited microbes. While cells of the digestive tract interact with gut microbes, root cells cut deals with soil microbes. The human world and the botanical world share a common theme—lots of communication and exchanges with microbes.

But the common thread linking the gut and the root runs deeper yet. Our teeth do the work of soil detritivores, chomping and chewing away at organic matter to make it smaller, which allows other organisms to continue the decomposition process. Stomach acids function like the fungal acids in soils, breaking food down into absorbable molecules. The small intestine absorbs nutrients much the same way plant roots absorb nutrients dissolved in water. And the inside of the small intestine is carpeted with small, thread-like projections called microvilli that increase the surface area many times over, greatly increasing nutrient absorption—just like root hairs in the soil.[16]

16   *The Hidden Half of Nature: The Microbial Roots of Life and Health*, David Montgomery and Anne Biklé (W.W. Norton & Company, 2016) p. 244

The reference to "root cells cutting deals with soil microbes" is striking. I would have imagined symbiosis to be less a process of dealing and more a process of sharing. I'm already wondering who is cornering the market on REOs (root exudate obligations), who is arbitraging PGPRs (plant growth promoting rhizobacteria), and who is buying the market of MCBs (microbial community bonds)... only to burrow my way to the *American Journal of Botany*, where researchers report, much to my surprise:

> Mycorrhizal symbiotic relationships are governed by an equal exchange of nutrients and benefits for each member (Kiers et al. 2011). For example, it was observed in experiments with *Medicago truncatula Gaertn.* that as more carbon was given to the mycorrhizal partner, the mycorrhiza in turn provided the plant with more phosphorous (Kiers et al. 2011). This "fair-trade" between plant and mycorrhiza also occurs with respect to N, as then the mycorrhiza only provides the plant with N when it receives plant carbon (Fellbaum et al. 2012). In other words, both members of the relationship need to benefit.[17]

And if you are extremely good at burrowing through sidenotes, try this one.[18]

17   *Rhizosphere Interactions: Root Exudates, Microbes, and Microbial Communities,* Huang, Chaparro, Reardon, Zhang, Shen and Vivanco (*Botany,* vol. 92, 2014)

18   "Plant root exudates mediate a multitude of rhizospheric interactions: at the species level (right side of schematic), multitrophic interactions (bottom), and at the community level (left side of schematic). The rhizospheric microbial community structure changes depending upon: (1) plant genotype (Broeckling et al. 2008; Bulgarelli et al. 2012; Lundberg et al. 2012; Micallef et al. 2009*a*, 2009*b*), (2) plant developmental stage (Chaparro et al. 2013*b*; İnceoğlu et al. 2011; Micallef et al. 2009*a*), (3) exposure to disease-suppressive soils (Mendes et al. 2011), (4) root exudate composition (Badri et al. 2009*a*, 2013*a*), and (5) plant hormone signaling (Carvalhais et al. 2013). Specific compounds released as root exudates mediate one-to-one, plant–microbe, or species-level interactions: (6) flavonoids act as signaling compounds to initiate symbiosis between legumes and rhizobia (Abdel-Lateif et al. 2012), (7) strigolactones stimulate mycorrhizal hyphal branching (Akiyama et al. 2005), (8) malic acid is involved in recruiting specific plant-growth-promoting rhizobacteria (PGPR) (*Bacillus subtilis*) (Rudrappa et al. 2008), (9) disruption or initiation of quorum sensing (QS) in bacteria (Gao et al. 2003), and (10) sugars and amino acids act as chemoattractants for microbes (Somers et al. 2004). The roles of (11) proteins secreted by roots and their inter-action with other organisms in the rhizosphere is very limited and needs further exploration to conclusively determine the mechanisms at play (De-la-Peña et al. 2008; Mathesius 2009). Other root exudates mediate multitrophic interactions: (12) plants attract nematodes, which act as carriers of rhizobia to the roots to increase nodulation (Horiuchi et al. 2005), (13) plant-growth-promoting rhizo-bacteria (PGPR) and rhizobia interaction result in the increase of nodulation efficiency (Guiñazú et al. 2010), and (14) PGPR interaction with mycorrhizae increase colonization efficiency (Hernandez and Chailloux 2004; Vosátka and Gryndler 1999). Different rods represent different microbial taxon. Each grey rectangle (left side) represents a distinct rhizosphere microbial community; different colored rods within each community represent the qualitative and quantitative distribution of microbes. Squares, pentagons, circles, stars, and rectangles represent different compounds released as root exudates." (*Botany,* Huang et. al.)

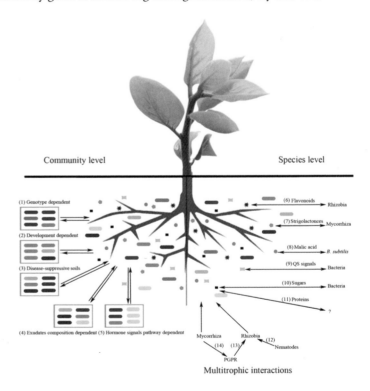

Community level   Species level

(1) Genotype dependent

(2) Development dependent

(3) Disease-suppressive soils

(4) Exudates composition dependent   (5) Hormone signals pathway dependent

(6) Flavonoids — Rhizobia
(7) Strigolactones — Mycorrhiza
(8) Malic acid — *B. subtilis*
(9) QS signals — Bacteria
(10) Sugars — Bacteria
(11) Proteins — ?

Mycorrhiza   Rhizobia
(14)   (13)   (12) — Nematodes
PGPR

Multitrophic interactions

"Fair trade" between plant roots and soil microbes?

Living, as we do, in an era dominated by Deal Doers—with Do Gooders often relegated to the remote provinces (along with Luddites, Malthusians, De-Growthers, Occupiers, folks who are on the wrong side of the right wall or the right side of the wrong wall or just this side of the last memories of the Berlin Wall, future Uber drivers, unionistas, trustafarians, rabbis who perform interfaith marriages, Muslims who agree with Henry Ford on the subject of finance,[19] refuseniks, peaceniks, beetniks,[20] Code Pinkos, and others of various rainbow predilections)—one can only imagine what kind of fair trade deals the actinomycetes are cutting with the nematodes.

* * * * *

I'm not sure why anyone would compare something as elegant as soil fertility to the business of global trade. But, clearly, some do. So, let's run with it for a few moments.

According to the World Fair Trade Organization:

> Fair Trade is a trading partnership, based on dialogue, transparency and respect, that seeks greater equity in international trade. It contributes to sustainable development by offering better trading conditions to, and securing the rights of, marginalized producers and workers—especially in the South. Fair Trade Organizations, backed by consumers, are engaged actively in supporting producers, awareness raising and in campaigning for changes in the rules and practice of conventional international trade.

Fair Trade is reintroducing a human face into the global production, processing, and distribution of agricultural goods. Direct relationships between producer and consumer have been sacrificed in pursuit of cheap, shelf-stable food; Fair Trade seeks to reintegrate some of these relationships into the supply chain, allowing consumers to value social and environmental factors that get squeezed out of the commodity equation.

While Fair Trade continues to increase its market share, it remains a small fraction of overall trade. In 2015, 179,119 metric tons of certified Fair Trade coffee were sold internationally, out of total global coffee production of some 9 million tons. The orders of magnitude are similar for cocoa, bananas, tea, rice, sugar, and flowers.

19 Ford stated that fixed interest on business loans, determined "according to some scale that has no bearing upon the particular business in which the money has been placed [...] is at the root of most business failures [...] Any return should come after it has produced, not before." For full citation, see *Inquiries into the Nature of Slow Money*, p. 67.

20 Slow Money has hosted a few on-line Beetcoin campaigns, through which a total of $169,474 was raised for 6 small food enterprises from 758 beetniks.

Meanwhile, everywhere there is fertile soil, a "multitude of rhizospheric interactions" goes about its intimate business.

("Fair Trade, Shmair Trade," no enterprising mycorrhizal fungus ever said.)

* * * * *

A few years ago, I got a call from *New York Times* reporter Ron Lieber, who writes for the Your Money column.

"My next column," he told me, "is going to be called 'Investing For The Truly Fed Up'. I can't tell you how many folks I hear from who don't want to invest in the military or sweatshops or tobacco or gambling or nuclear power, and now there's a whole new wave of folks who are adding fossil fuel to the list. I came across Slow Money recently. Many of these same fed up folks are interested in organics. So, my question is: For those who want to avoid all those bad things, and who are interested in organics and local food, but who still need to make 7% on their retirement account, what does Slow Money have to offer?"

"Ron, I was right with you up until the 7%," I replied. "If you really believe in avoiding that litany of things you listed, then you can't end the sentence with, 'But I need to make 7%.' When it comes to certain things, you need to stop doing the numbers the 20th century way."

I could include, here, a litany of financial statistics that fiduciaries use to analyze the risk and return of investments and another litany of social and environmental statistics that fiduciaries, following their fiduciary duty, generally feel compelled to exclude.

But this is not about numbers—doing these numbers vs. doing those numbers. This is about reaffirming the primacy of words over the claims on our attention made by numbers. Reaffirming the primacy of relationships over the claims of transactions. Reaffirming the primacy of nutrition over the claims of cheap calories. Reaffirming the primacy of places over the claims of markets. Reaffirming the primacy of generations and seasons over the claims of milliseconds and algorithms. Reaffirming the primacy of putting back in over the claims of taking out.

* * * * *

Words over numbers. Take the title of this book:

SOIL
2017

M.C. Escher, Day and Night

Literally, a word over a number. Look closely and you'll see that they are almost reversed images of one another. Flip SOIL down, on its head, and it almost turns into 2017 (but the L makes a backwards 7). Not quite a figure/ground *trompe l'oeil*, but a curious visual serendipity, nonetheless. Vaguely Escheresque.

Graphic artist M.C. Escher gained considerable fame in the mid-twentieth century for his symmetrical designs and figure/ground images. His work is a kind of ultra-sophisticated visual primal scream, warning that we must not let the conventional way of seeing things have sovereignty over our thoughts. Escher used elements of perspective, architecture, and symmetry to integrate the possible and the impossible; staircases that lead up and down at the same time, floors that are also ceilings, planes that seem three-dimensional, patterns that merge living things and geometric forms. He joined dualities in overarching unities. You can see, at the extremes, fish and fowl and day and night as being wholly separate, yet at the center Escher's aesthetic holds them together, makes them one, suggesting an ethos of intimate connection and interdependence.

M.C. Escher, Encounter

Figure meets ground meets biology meets geometry meets quantity meets quality meets here meets there meets technique meets enigma.

I was intrigued to discover the following passage from Escher's 1953 lecture to Friends of the Stedelijk Museum in Alkmaar:

> It may seem paradoxical to say that there are similarities between a poetical and a commercial mind, but it is a fact that both a poet and businessman are constantly dealing with problems that are directly related to people [...] The business-like mind is sometimes described as being cold, sober, calculating, hard, but perhaps these are simply qualities that are necessary for dealing with people if one wants to achieve anything. One is always concerned with the mysterious, incalculable, dark, hidden aspects for which there is no easy formula, but which form essentially the same human element as that which inspires the poet.[21]

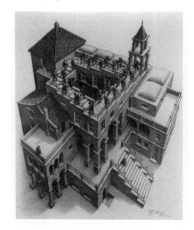

M.C. Escher, Ascending and Descending

21   *M.C. Escher: His Life and Complete Graphic Work,* Bool, Kist, Locher, and Wierda (Harry N. Abrams, 1982) p. 73

His conclusion about what is necessary in business leaves me with many questions, but we can all agree that computer algorithms and derivatives and ultra-fast trading are, particularly to the layperson (but, also unfortunately, too often to the highly-incentivized financial professional), "mysterious, incalculable, dark, hidden aspects for which there is no easy formula." Business as figure, poetry as ground—it would seem that there is no duality that Escher could not fuse into an overarching unity.

And, so, I would like to offer for his posthumous consideration the following as a figure/ground stumper: Industrial food systems. Industrial food systems are a figure without a ground. CAFOs,[22] GMOs,[23] NPK,[24] high fructose corn syrup, Roundup, mouthfeel texturants, Polysorbate 80, transfats, Yellow Dye Number Whatever, feedlots, manure lagoons, Cocoa Puffs, untold BTUs spent processing, distributing, refrigerating, and freezing food—these all are part of a figure that has no ground.

And a figure without a ground, like a house divided, cannot stand.

* * * * *

Escher's work brings me back to the late sixties and early seventies. His play with perspective seemed particularly apropos for a time that was questioning convention on so many levels, birthing a wave of social change movements that generally went by the name *counterculture*. Civil Rights. Women's Lib. Gay Rights. The Vietnam War as figure; the peace movement as ground. Levittown as figure; communes as ground. There were the assassinations of JFK, MLK Jr., and RFK. East was meeting west, sitar meeting guitar. Woodstock, the first Earth Day, the Uncola, moon rocks, Pet Rocks,[25] Watergate, the OPEC oil embargo. In the years following all this ruckus, in roughly the same wave of thought leadership as E.F. Schumacher and Wendell Berry, Christopher Alexander and a team of co-authors from the University of California at Berkeley published a tour de force called *A Pattern Language*, an architectural vision celebrating appropriate scale, organic relationships between built environment and landscape, and design that comes alive by engendering a sense of belonging. Alexander could have been describing M.C. Escher:

> No pattern is an isolated entity. Each pattern can exist in the world, only to the extent that is supported by other patterns: the larger patterns in which it is embedded, the patterns of the same size that surround it, and the smaller patterns which are embedded in it.

> This is a fundamental view of the world. It says that when you build a thing you cannot merely build that thing in isolation, but must also repair the world around it, and within it, so that the larger world at that one place becomes more

22 CAFOs, or confined animal feeding operations, of the kind described in the preceding *TIME* magazine article. A CAFO confines thousands of hogs in barns, each, say, with a half-acre footprint. In contrast, Paul Willis, who oversees Niman Ranch operations in Iowa, raises 1,000 hogs outside on 150 acres of pasture. A pound of Oscar Mayer bacon costs $6.99 at King Sooper's in Boulder, Colorado; a pound of Niman Ranch bacon costs $10.64 at Alfalfa's Local Market in Boulder.

23 Genetically Modified Organisms—perhaps the most hotly debated aspect of industrial agriculture. While, for centuries, plant breeders have selectively bred plant varieties for desired properties, only recently have they developed the capacity to splice fish genes into tomatoes in order to enhance frost resistance, or to genetically modify corn in order to render it, in Monsanto's lingo, "Roundup Ready," that is, resistant to glyphosate, the active ingredient in Monsanto's herbicide Roundup.

24 NPK stands for nitrogen, phosphorus, and potassium, the trinity of components in chemical fertilizer.

25 "Dahl's quirky brainchild became a phenomenon, selling more than 1 million Pet Rocks at $4 apiece. *TIME* called the cleverly packaged novelty '1% product and 99% marketing genius.' It hit the market at an opportune moment. A president had resigned, the Vietnam War had ended and the nation was ready for a giggle. 'This takes them on a fantasy trip—you might say we've packaged a sense of humor,' Dahl told *People* magazine in 1975. With tongue firmly planted in cheek, he offered plenty of hilarity. In a section on tricks, for example, Dahl's spoof manual informed owners that the Pet Rock can roll over—as long as it is attempting the feat on a hill." (Gary Dahl dies at 78; creator of Pet Rock, 1970s pop culture icon, *Los Angeles Times*, April 1, 2015)

coherent, and more whole; and the thing which you make takes its place in the web of nature, as you make it.[26]

26   *A Pattern Language*, Christopher Alexander et. al. (Oxford University Press, 1977) p. xiii

He also could have been describing a small, diversified, organic farm. In the essay "Solving for Pattern," Wendell Berry pulls this mosaic together:

> The farmer has put plants and animals into a relationship of mutual dependence, and must perforce be concerned for balance or symmetry, a reciprocating connection in the pattern of the farm that is biological, not industrial, and that involves solutions to problems of fertility, soil husbandry, economics, sanitation—a whole complex of problems whose proper solutions add up to *health*: the health of the soil, of plants and animals, of farm and farmer, of farm family and farm community, all involved in the same internested, interlocking pattern—or pattern of patterns.[27]

27   *The Gift of Good Land*, Wendell Berry, (North Point Press, 1981) p. 137

A healthy farm, of the kind Berry describes, connects us not only to living systems, but also to that pattern of patterns known as history. A healthy farm is a living manifestation of lessons learned over millennia. Lessons about carrying capacity—the challenges of tending agricultural land without diminishing its fertility. Lessons about what happens when the industrial figure behaves as if the agrarian ground is expendable.

These lessons are still playing themselves out. In early November 2016, James Rebanks, a British sheep farmer, visited rural America for the first time and was shocked to see the degree to which modern agribusiness is killing the American Dream. His Op Ed in the *New York Times* bears inclusion in full:

> MATTERDALE, England — I am a traditional small farmer in the North of England. I farm sheep in a mountainous landscape, the Lake District fells. It is a farming system that dates back as many as 4,500 years. A remarkable survival. My flock grazes a mountain alongside 10 other flocks, through an ancient communal grazing system that has somehow survived the last two centuries of change. Wordsworth called it a "perfect republic of shepherds."
>
> It's not your efficient modern agribusiness. My farm struggles to make enough money for my family to live on, even with 900 sheep. The price of my lambs is governed by the supply of imported lamb from the other side of the world.

An abandoned building in Owsley County, Kentucky. (Appeared in Rebanks' *New York Times* piece.) *Mario Tama, Getty Images*

James Rebanks and sheep,
Lake District, Northern England

So, I have one foot in something ancient and the other foot in the 21st-century global economy.

Less than 3 percent of people in modern industrial economies are farmers. But around the world, I am not alone: The United Nations estimates that more than two billion people are farmers, most of them small farmers; that's about one in three people on the planet.

My farm's lack of profitability perhaps shouldn't be of any great concern to anyone else. I'm a grown-up, and I chose to live this way. I chose it because my ancestors all did this, and because I love it, however doomed it might seem to others.

My farm is where I live, and there is actually no other way to farm my land, which is why it hasn't changed much for a millennium or more. In truth, I could accept the changes around me philosophically, including the disappearance of farms like mine, if the results made for a better world and society. But the world I am seeing evolve in front of my eyes isn't better, it is worse. Much worse.

In the week before the United States elected Donald J. Trump to the presidency, I traveled through Kentucky, through endless miles of farmland and small towns. It was my first visit to the United States, for a book tour. I was shocked by the signs of decline I saw in rural America.

I saw shabby wood-frame houses rotting by the roadside, and picket fences blown over by the wind. I passed boarded-up shops in the hearts of small towns, and tumbledown barns and abandoned farmland. The church notice boards were full of offers of help to people with drug or alcohol addictions. And yes, suddenly I was passing cars with Trump stickers on their bumpers, and passing houses with Trump flags on their lawns.

The economic distress and the Trump support are not unconnected, of course. Significant areas of rural America are broken, in terminal economic decline, as food production heads off to someplace else where it can be done supposedly more efficiently. In many areas, nothing has replaced the old industries. This is a cycle of degeneration that puts millions of people on the wrong side of economic history.

Economists say that when the world changes people will adapt, move and change to fit the new world. But of course, real human beings often don't do that. They cling to the places they love, and their identity remains tied to the outdated or inefficient things they used to do, like being steel workers or farmers. Often, their skills are not transferable anyway, and they have no interest in the new opportunities. So, these people get left behind.

I ask myself what I would do if I didn't farm sheep, or if I couldn't any longer farm sheep. I have no idea.

Perhaps it is none of my business how Americans conduct their affairs and how they think about economics. I should doubtless go back to the mountains of my home here in Cumbria, and hold my tongue. But for my entire life, my own country has apathetically accepted an American model of farming and food retailing, mostly through a belief that it was the way of progress and the natural course of economic development. As a result, America's future is the default for us all.

It is a future in which farming and food have changed and are changing radically—in my view, for the worse. Thus, I look at the future with a skeptical eye. We have all become such suckers for a bargain that we take the low prices of our foodstuffs for granted and are somehow unable to connect these bargain-basement prices to our children's inability to find meaningful work at a decently paid job.

Our demand for cheap food is killing the American dream for millions of people. Among its side effects, it is creating terrible health problems like obesity and antibiotic-resistant infections, and it is destroying the habitats upon which wildlife depends. It also concentrates vast wealth and power in fewer and fewer hands.

After my trip to rural America, I returned to my sheep and my strangely old-fashioned life. I am surrounded by beauty, and a community, and an old way of doing things that has worked for a long time rather well. I have come home convinced that it is time to think carefully, both within America and without, about food and farming and what kind of systems we want.

> The future we have been sold doesn't work. Applying the principles of the factory floor to the natural world just doesn't work. Farming is more than a business. Food is more than a commodity. Land is more than a mineral resource.
>
> Despite the growing scale of the problem, no major mainstream politician has taken farming or food seriously for decades. With the presidential campaign over and a president in the White House whom rural Kentuckians helped elect, the new political establishment might want to think about this carefully.
>
> Suddenly, rural America matters. It matters for the whole world.[28]

28   *An English Sheep Farmer's View of Rural America,* James Rebanks (March 1, 2017, *New York Times* Opinion Pages)

It is well-nigh impossible, at this moment, for our attention not to rush directly to the reference to presidential politics, for our thinking not to be overwhelmed by a violent burst of despair at the crudeness of our political discourse and our inability to address issues at the heart of political dysfunction. But in Rebanks' words I hear a sadness that transcends politics. His is a meta-political sadness. This is the sadness of a returning in which we are all complicit. We keep returning, with an addictive compulsion, to the cab of the political bulldozer, rubbing our hands together and revving it up, in hopes of using it to plant seeds of meta-political healing.

*   *   *   *   *

In 1968, Robert F. Kennedy diagnosed this kind of meta-political, meta-economic sadness in his own way:

> We will find neither national purpose nor personal satisfaction in a mere continuation of economic progress, in an endless amassing of worldly goods. We cannot measure national spirit by the Dow Jones Average, nor national achievement by the Gross National Product. For the Gross National Product includes air pollution, and ambulances to clear our highways from carnage. It counts special locks for our doors and jails for the people who break them. The Gross National Product includes the destruction of the redwoods and the death of Lake Superior. It grows with the production of napalm and missiles and nuclear warheads [...] It includes [...] the broadcasting of television programs which glorify violence to sell goods to our children.

And if the Gross National Product includes all this, there is much that it does not comprehend. It does not allow for the health of our families, the quality of their education, or the joy of their play. It is indifferent to the decency of our factories and the safety of our streets alike. It does not include the beauty of our poetry, or the strength of our marriages, the intelligence of our public debate or the integrity of our public officials [...] The Gross National Product measures neither our wit nor our courage, neither our wisdom nor our learning, neither our compassion nor our devotion to our country. It measures everything, in short, except that which makes life worthwhile, and it can tell us everything about America—except why we are proud to be Americans.[29]

29   Speech at University of Kansas, March 18, 1968.

I, and many who are seeking alternative pathways to a healthier future, return frequently to these words. (Resulting, in my case, in frequent apologies to those who've heard me use them before.) An educational critic once offered that one of the problems with our schools is that they encourage rote learning, resulting in the attitude that each subject is isolated, something you *take* and that once you've *taken it*, you move on to the next subject, without understanding broader contexts. So, I am not embarrassed to keep returning to wisdom that I've encountered along the way and to continually reflect upon it, acknowledging the challenges it poses to my own actions.

I'd say RFK's words are comfort food for the metrics-and-rancor-weary, but they are more than that. Few public figures have ever captured as powerfully the sadness that comes from an overreliance on the numbers.

* * * * *

No discussion of the numbers, of financial return, of our expectations as investors and our connection to the larger economy whence our returns derive, can be complete without touching on GNP and its sister, GDP (Gross Domestic Product). They haven't been around all that long, although it seems like forever.

For thousands of years, economic growth was minimal. The following chart (see margin) shows that from roughly the dawn of agriculture (give or take 5,000 years) to the 19th century, per capita GDP around the world barely grew. Then, as industrialization took hold, economic growth sped up dramatically, with per capita GDP increasing roughly 50 times between the 19th and 21st centuries. There were booms and busts and panics aplenty along the way, but economies were still relatively decentralized, with major rural components and a large percentage of the population living on small farms.

HISTORICAL PER CAPITA GDP GROWTH

Year	Population (in millions)	GDP per capita (in year 2000 dollars)
5000 BCE	5	$130
1000 BCE	50	$160
1	170	$135
1000	265	$165
1500	425	$175
1800	900	$250
1900	1625	$850
1950	2515	$2030
1975	4080	$4640
2000	6120	$8175
2010	6896	$9037

The Little Big Number: How GDP Came to Rule the World and What to Do About It, Dirk Philipsen (Princeton University Press, 2015) p. 69

In 1820, 79% of the American workforce was engaged in farming, 93% of the U.S. population lived in rural areas, and GDP was $12.5 billion. In 1910, 31% of the workforce was farming, 54% of Americans lived in rural areas, and GDP approached $500 billion. Today, 2% of the U.S. workforce is involved in farming, 15% of the population lives in rural areas, and GDP is $18 trillion.[30]

With increasing urbanization and industrialization, and the dependence of urban populations on manufacturing jobs and purchasing power, grew the need for better understanding of national income and unemployment. But it was the advent of the Great Depression, and later, World War II, that brought new urgency to the task of developing consistent measures of economic growth and a system of tracking national income and productivity.

Economist Simon Kuznets and his team developed the national income account which, after the war, became known as Gross National Product and, then, Gross Domestic Product—a single number summarizing the output of the economy and serving as a metric of economic growth. Deciding how and what to count was the subject of considerable debate among economists and policy makers. Kuznets himself warned Congress that "the valuable capacity of the human mind to simplify a complex situation in a compact characterization becomes dangerous," anticipating the distortions that could arise from metrics that were narrowly focused on economic growth.

His concerns have since been echoed and amplified by many:

> It's hard to imagine a time in which national economies were not measured by GDP. Today, the tyranny of ignorance that characterized modern economics into the 1930s and helped bring about the Great Depression has been replaced by another kind of tyranny, that of a single metric [...]

> Values that had developed over thousands of years in many different cultural contexts were largely abandoned within a generation. In a process that started with industrialization and came to full fruition after World War II, value itself came to be determined in ways that challenged core global traditions, from the nature of work to the meaning of human existence.

> Quality of life itself or what the American tradition more precisely frames as the quality of *life, liberty, and the pursuit of happiness,* has no defined space in the pursuit of growth—it is not recognized as a category in our national and international economic ledgers. As such, our economic goals are fundamentally out of sync with our political and cultural achievements.[31]

30   Two thirds of total American farm revenue is generated today by the largest 76,000 farms, or 3.8 percent of all farms—those with 2,000 acres or more. In 1900, there were 5.7 million U.S. farms, average size 147 acres; in 2012, there were 2.1 million farms, average size 434 acres. (USDA, 2012 Census of Agriculture, and Statista, 2017)

COST OF MAKING A FARM, WESTERN NEW YORK STATE, 1821

$300	Clearing 30 acres at $10 per acre
$70	Fencing
$200	Log house and frame barn
$150	Outhouse, well, orchard
$50	1 pair oxen
$50	1 horse
$40	2 cows
$10	2 hogs
$50	10 sheep
$50	Plow, harness, tools
$100	Purchase 50 acres at $2 per acre
$75	Essentials for family consumption before first crop
$1,145	**Total**

Digital History 2016

31   Philipsen p. 12–13

GDP is an undiscriminating measurement of dollar flows, treating all dollars as equal, which sounds value-neutral at first, and, therefore, perfectly reasonable—until you realize that dollars flowing due to the spill of a CAFO lagoon or building stealth bombers or selling cigarettes are not the same, in terms of their relationship to the well-being of people and communities, as dollars flowing to school lunch programs or local newspapers or community health clinics.

* * * * *

A small movement has emerged in recent years to develop alternatives to GDP. One is the Genuine Progress Indicator (GPI), which separates *goods* from *ills*, distinguishing between economic activities that enhance social and environmental capital and those that diminish them. While there are many opportunities for disagreement with respect to the specifics of various metrics within the GPI, the overall picture it presents does comport with what millions of Americans are sensing: GDP is in some ways diverging from our well-being.

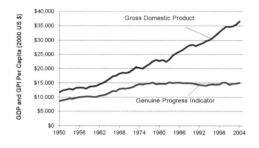

Comparison of GDP and GPI per Capita, United States, 1950–2004

GPI's assessment of 26 variables related to economic, social, and environmental progress—everything from the value of housework and volunteerism to the cost of crime and loss of farmland—portrays a widening gap between economic growth and genuine progress. We have created wealth, but along with it has come increasing political, cultural, and ecological dysfunction. The stock market goes up, but so does wealth inequality, opioid use, and carbon in the atmosphere. The average monthly cost of cancer drugs goes from $2,000 in 2000 to $11,325 in 2014—GDP goes up.[32] Fifty-nine Tomahawk missiles fired into Syria—GDP up.[33] New pre-mudded jeans sell for $425 a pair—GDP up.[34]

The formula for computing GDP is deceptively simple:

$$GDP = Consumption + Private\ Investment + Government\ Spending + (Exports - Imports)$$

The aggregate number that is produced by these calculations is as opaque as it is reductionist, however, and its connection to our daily lives, to the health of households, communities, and bioregions, is increasingly tenuous.

Similarly, with the Dow Jones Industrial Average. We celebrate its rise, but how about also asking: *What's in it?* I've asked many times in public discussions, "Who knows how many companies are in the DJIA? Can anyone name them?" Only sporadically, in rooms filled with many thousands of folks in the aggregate, are partial answers forthcoming. Which belies deeper questioning of the RFK kind: How

32   Carolyn Y. Johnson, *Washington Post*, May 2, 2016

33   Each Tomahawk missile costs approximately $1 million.

34   Barracuda Jeans, recently featured at Nordstrom, are described thus: "Heavily distressed medium-blue denim jeans in a comfortable straight-leg fit embody rugged, Americana workwear that's seen some hard-working action with a crackled, caked-on muddy coating that shows you're not afraid to get down and dirty."

much of the market value of these companies is tied to weapons manufacturing? Superfund sites? Junk food? Farmland succumbing to subdivisions?

* * * * *

There are quite a few initiatives working to develop healthier alternatives to GDP, including the Human Development Index, the Beyond GDP initiative, projects of the Club of Rome, the Food Sustainability Index, Capital Institute's work on Regenerative Capitalism, the Happy Planet Index, and Bhutan's Gross National Happiness index.

The United Nations' Human Development Index is a country-by-country summary measurement of life expectancy, education level, and standard of living; it has no environmental component. The European Commission's Beyond GDP initiative does not seek to replace GDP, but to supplement it with social, environmental, and wellbeing indicators. The Club of Rome, whose groundbreaking and controversial book *Limits to Growth* (1973) framed much of the contemporary environmental discussion, has a project called Reclaim Economics and a report called "Is Systemic Economic Change Possible Without Collapse?"

The Capital Institute's paper, "Regenerative Capitalism," by John Fullerton, presents a comprehensive revisioning of economics, seeking to "catalyze the paradigm shift away from today's flawed form of capitalism—one that is unjust and unsustainable—to a healthy, pluralistic system of regenerative economies aligned with the patterns of regenerative health." This unusual and extremely thoughtful work presents a successful Wall Street investment banker's quest for a whole new economic story.

In 2006, the New Economics Foundation introduced the Happy Planet Index:

- **Wellbeing:** How satisfied the residents of each country say they feel with life overall, on a scale from zero to ten, based on data collected as part of the Gallup World Poll.

- **Life Expectancy:** The average number of years a person is expected to live in each country based on data collected by the United Nations.

- **Inequality of Outcomes:** The inequalities between people within a country, in terms of how long they live, and how happy they feel, based on the distribution in each country's life expectancy and wellbeing data. Inequality of outcomes is expressed as a percentage.

A diagram of The Happy Planet Index

Ecological Footprint: The average impact that each resident of a country places on the environment, based on data prepared by the Global Footprint Network. Ecological Footprint is expressed using a standardized unit: global hectares (GHA) per person.[35]

35   http://neweconomics.org/

The U.S. currently scores 20.7 out of a 100 on the HPI scale, ranking 108th out of 140 countries measured.

There's also an index that focuses on food and agriculture. It's called the Food Sustainability Index, developed by the Barilla Center for Food and Nutrition:

> The Food Sustainability Index is a ranking of 25 countries on food system sustainability. It was created as a quantitative and qualitative benchmarking model, constructed from 58 indicators that measure the sustainability of food systems across three themes: Food Loss and Waste, Sustainable Agriculture, and Nutritional Challenges. The index contains three types of key performance indicators: environmental, societal, and economic.[36]

36   http://barillacfn.com/

Our quick flyover of economic metrics and paradigms ends in Bhutan, which famously uses its own Gross National Happiness index. GNH measures 33 categories within nine overall domains: psychological wellbeing, health, education, time use, cultural diversity and resilience, good governance, community vitality, ecological diversity and resilience, and living standards. The government administers a survey every four years and computes GNH based on responses. "The 2010 survey found that 10.4% of the population was 'unhappy' (defined as achieving sufficiency in 50% or less of the weighted indicators), 48.7% was 'narrowly happy,' 32.6% was 'extensively happy,' and 8.3% of the population was 'deeply happy' (showing sufficiency in 77% or more of the weighted indicators)."[37]

37   Gil Press, *Forbes*, September 15, 2015

The 2015 GNH findings describe the cultural context within which the Bhutanese developed their index:

> The quest for a better economic system, in harmony with nature and other sentient beings, resurfaced around the world. The unequal world that faced human beings made global leaders take a longer pause for thought. Equity is an ingredient of happiness, particularly when people think of their material standing in comparison to others, notwithstanding the fact that everyone may be becoming better off. It was also noticed that not only poverty but prosperity has made people more harried, time-scarce, and stressed, and miss the pleasures of slowness. Social scientists' observation of the poor correlation between life

satisfaction and economic growth among a substantial section of the world was another new finding that echoed the GNH.

Economies are unstable because the markets, both abroad and domestic, expand and contract. Markets are volatile for several reasons. Products are changing in quality and the locations of their production move around the world looking for cheaper costs of production. Such flux in economies is reflected in the compulsion to update the content of education aimed at renewing competencies and overcoming competition in the market place. The quality of products changes due to innovations, some of which are excellent while others appeal to the artificial needs of human beings. The distinction between artificial and authentic needs is largely dependent on the psychological stability of the consumers. If the consumers are unable to develop any consistency and stability in their psychology over time, no consumer good would be seen as good enough for long enough.

Exceptionalism comes in many flavors. Bhutanese exceptionalism is based on the pleasures of slowness and psychological stability, rather than on social mobility, technological innovation, consumerism, and military power.

The idea that Bhutan and a British think tank are developing ways to measure national happiness should make us happy—but only up to a point.

Amalgamating qualitative concerns into a set of numbers, much less a single number, is, in some fundamental respects, at odds with the very happiness we are so desirous of pursuing. It's a little like Heisenberg's Uncertainty Principle in physics, which stipulates that we cannot measure both a particle's mass and its velocity with precision—the very process of measurement influences them, and the more accurately we know one, the less accurately we know the other. In the process of measuring happiness, monetization, economic metrics, and indices are influencing Bhutan, just as they influence those parts of our own inner landscapes that need to be left "a little wild," to use John Maynard Keynes' oft-cited phrase.

* * * * *

Like many others who've come across it, I've been intrigued for quite a while by Keynes' statement, "Words ought to be a little wild, for they are the assault of thoughts on the unthinking." This morning, as I paused to consider them once I again, I found myself wondering: When had he said this? What was the context?

I had to scroll through a few Google pages—dozens of folks feature this quote on their website, but do so without any source. Eventually, I found Keynes' 1933 speech:

I see three outstanding dangers in economic nationalism [...]

The first is Silliness—the silliness of the doctrinaire. It is nothing strange to discover this in movements which have passed somewhat suddenly from the phase of midnight high-flown talk into the field of action. We do not distinguish, at first, between the color of the rhetoric with which we have won a people's assent and the dull substance of the truth of our message. There is nothing insincere in the transition. Words ought to be a little wild—for they are the assault of thoughts upon the unthinking. But when the seats of power and authority have been attained, there should be no more poetic license [...]

When a doctrinaire proceeds to action, he must, so to speak, forget his doctrine. For those who in action remember the letter will probably lose what they are seeking.

The second danger—and a worse danger than silliness—is Haste. Paul Valery's aphorism is worth quoting: "Political conflicts distort and disturb the people's sense of distinction between matters of importance and matters of urgency." The economic transition of a society is a thing to be accomplished slowly. What I have been discussing is not a sudden revolution, but the direction of secular trend. We have a fearful example in Russia to-day of the evils of insane and unnecessary haste. The sacrifices and losses of transition will be vastly greater if the pace is forced [...] For it is of the nature of economic processes to be rooted in time. A rapid transition will involve so much pure destruction of wealth that the new state of affairs will be, at first, far worse than the old; and the grand experiment will be discredited [...]

The third risk, and the worst risk of all three, is Intolerance and the stifling of in-structed criticism. The new movements have usually come into power through a phase of violence or quasi-violence. They have not convinced their opponents; they have downed them. It is the modern method—but very disastrous, I am still old-fashioned enough to believe—to depend on propaganda and to seize the organs of opinion; it is thought to be clever and useful to fossilize thought and to use all the forces of authority to paralyze the play of mind on mind. For those who have found it necessary to employ all methods whatever to attain power, it is a serious temptation to continue to use for the task of construction the same dangerous tools which wrought the preliminary housebreaking.

Russia, again, furnishes us with an example of the crushing blunders which a régime makes when it has exempted itself from criticism [...] We all hate criticism. Nothing but rooted principle will cause us willingly to expose ourselves to it.

Yet the new economic modes, towards which we are blundering, are, in the essence of their nature, experiments. We have no clear idea laid up in our minds beforehand of exactly what we want. We shall discover it as we move along, and we shall have to mould our material in accordance with our experience. Now for this process, bold, free, and remorseless criticism is a *sine qua non* of ultimate success.[38]

38   "National Self-Sufficiency," a speech delivered by John Maynard Keynes at University College Dublin, April 19, 1933

John Maynard Keynes, one of the 20th century's most influential economists, talking eight decades ago about economic nationalism, Russia, and the need for slow economic experimentation.

* * * * *

I kept foraging and his words got wilder, still. *AHA!:*

We have until recently conceived it a moral duty to ruin the tillers of the soil and destroy the age-long human traditions attendant on husbandry, if we could get a loaf of bread thereby a tenth of a penny cheaper. There was nothing which it was not our duty to sacrifice to this Moloch and Mammon in one; for we faithfully believed that the worship of these monsters would overcome the evil of poverty and lead the next generation safely and comfortably, on the back of compound interest, into economic peace.

Artists, farmers, poets, philosophers, even the occasional politician, have been evoking truth and beauty, this way and that, for hundreds, even thousands of years. Now, here was an economist, not just any economist, but John Maynard Keynes, the father of modern macroeconomics, telling us all we ever need to know about the tension between economics and health, faith, and peace. He got to the tillers of the soil and to the cost of bread, but he didn't quite get to the soil itself and all that lives therein.

That's where we come in.

* * * * *

We are the we who are willing to pay that tenth of a penny, that penny, perhaps, even, that ten cents or more. We may or may not be Keynesians, but we are people who recognize the meta-economics of a good loaf of bread. We are the we who are willing to swing from Keynes to one Crescent Dragonwagon, confident enough in our own common sense to know from which to seek economic direction and from which to seek an actual loaf of bread.[39] Author of 50 books, including James Beard award-winning *Passionate Vegetarian* and 29 children's books, Dragonwagon, who was for a time Julia Child's writing teacher, wrote in 1968: "Baking a loaf of brown bread in this society is revolutionary, if you know why you're doing it." She no doubt did not envision the emergence of the brown bread industry.

In 2010, for the first time, sales of whole wheat bread surpassed those of white bread—$2.6 billion compared with $2.5 billion. However, the imperatives of large-scale industrial production and distribution make the mass-produced brown bread of today something to which the word *revolution* cannot reasonably be applied. Most of the pre-sliced brown breads that you find wrapped in plastic on supermarket shelves contain, just like their white-loaf counterparts, such additives as benzoyl peroxide, potassium bromate, azodicarbonamide, calcium propionate, sweeteners, something called DATEM (diacetyl tartaric acid ester of mono- and diglycerides, a.k.a. food additive E472e), natamycin, and/or more. These are the kind of ingredients that make it possible for a 20-ounce loaf of Wonder Bread to be mass produced, have stable shelf life, and sell for $2.39.

Compared to this, a $10, 2½ pound loaf of Babettes bread seems expensive, and a $13 organic sourdough spelt Shepherd's Loaf seems downright anti-democratic.[40] It's easy to forget, when confronted with artisan-bread sticker shock, that the cheap stuff is made without fermentation (that is, made quickly, using industrially produced yeast, rather than made slowly, from naturally occurring yeast), contains all those chemicals, and, for good measure, has a crust that is so soft and tasteless that the word *crust* is about as appropriate as the words *revolution* or *wonder*.

La Brea Bakery in Los Angeles is steering a middle course, seeking to preserve key parts of the artisan story while operating at an industrial scale. They are producing and distributing 40,000–50,000 pounds of bread and pastries per day, while sourcing heirloom organic wheat, respecting slow rising time, and using no preservatives. Is it possible to be "the world's largest artisan baker" or is that a little too much like HSBC's positioning, which it eventually abandoned, as "the world's local bank"? Aaron Bobrow-Strain describes his visit to La Brea's manufacturing facility:

> La Brea's Van Nuys plant is an M.C. Escher optical illusion come to life: impossibly long lines of dough trailing into the visual vanishing point, becoming

39   "At sixteen, I got married for the first time. My then-husband-to-be and I thought that the woman should not take the man's last name, so we decided to choose a new last name. As I recall, somewhere in there we looked at one of those 'One Thousand Names for the Baby' books, and discovered that our old first names had meanings we did not agree with. His old first name, Mark, meant 'the warrior'; we were anti-war. My old first name, Ellen, meant 'the Queen'; we were anti-authoritarian. It was the '60's; we didn't agree with much. He came up with the new first names for us: Crispin, for him, meaning 'the curly-headed one'; Crescent, for me, meaning 'the growing.' The wedding drew nearer. We still hadn't come up with a new last name. One day, after trying and discarding several possibilities, I said, 'Maybe we're taking ourselves too seriously, maybe we should pick something completely frivolous.' He said, 'Like what?' I said, 'Oh, um, uh, like Dragonwagon.' Thus we became Crescent and Crispin Dragonwagon. If I had had any *idea* how many countless thousands of times I would have to explain this ridiculous name, I would have chosen something a lot less flashy. But by the time I realized how long the remainder of my days might be, and that I'd be pulling it around like a ball and chain, I already had a couple of books out and the start of a professional reputation. But, I will say it's a great children's book name; kids love saying it." (From dragonwagon.com) *Words ought to be a little wild...*

40   Of the latter, produced over two days, using a double-rise process, fifth-generation baker Tom Herbert of the Hobbs House Bakery in Nailsworth, Gloucestershire, England, says: "It is a work of art. I use a special flour called spelt that was brought to Britain by the Romans, a natural yeast called sourdough and Cotswold spring water. It's definitely Britain's most expensive loaf and I know it may seem horrifically overpriced but when you taste it you really know the difference. 90 per cent of bread is mass-produced and shouldn't technically be called bread at all." (Nick Collins, *The Telegraph*, June 9, 2010)

White Bread: A Social History of the Store-Bought Loaf, Aaron Bobrow-Strain (Beacon Press, 2012) p. 53. "White bread was, for the counterculture, an instructive commodity—a familiar, accessible way to comprehend any of the binaries that gave shape to the movement and animated revolt: authentic vs. artificial, natural vs. chemical, brown vs. white, healthy vs. poisonous, real vs. plastic, peaceful vs. militaristic [...] The sterile, chemically-laced, and homogenous substance of white bread could stand in as a synecdoche for social conformism, the environmental costs of industrialism, racism, bland suburbia, or cultural imperialism abroad. Establishment archenemies such as Robert McNamara or Earl Butz weren't *like* white bread, they *were* white bread." p. 167

42   *Letter to a Young Farmer: How to Live Richly without Wealth on the New Garden Farm*, Gene Logsdon (Chelsea Green, 2017) p. 19

43   Logsdon, p. 39

impossibly perfect squares, rolling themselves into perfectly uniform baguettes, marching off in impossibly long lines again, rotating into towering Ferris wheel contraptions, filing around corners, parading through tunnels, and spiraling up almost forty feet in the air. When the 80 percent-baked baguettes finally descend to earth, it is through the machine that makes La Brea's far-flung distribution possible: a massive blast freezer that inserts fresh, preservative-free bread into the global food system.[41]

The ShopRite website features a 10½ ounce La Brea Baguette for $2.49. "The dream of good bread for the masses," observes Bobrow-Strain, "is the most ancient of bread dreams."

How do we find our way, then, between the too cheap and the too expensive, the too industrial and the too artisanal? Western civilization has been wondering about the Golden Mean for a few thousand years, now.

Matters of scale, cost, and commercial viability are equally elusive when it comes to farming. Eliot Coleman and Jean-Martin Fortier lead the way for a new generation of micro-farms, grossing $100,000 or more from an acre or two of micro-greens and organic vegetables. Yet, living off the profits of a small farm is a goal most farmers cannot attain. In *Letter to a Young Farmer: How to Live Richly without Wealth on the New Garden Farm*, Gene Logsdon describes unapologetically—no, celebrates—the need for off-farm income, almost as a kind of litmus of the degree to which "the artisanal garden farm" is staying true to its biological and cultural values: "Real-money profits from farming just come in too slowly to live with our industrial, money-interest economy. The modern notion that it is beneath a real farmer's dignity to have another job is something left over from the landed aristocracy of the Middle Ages. Almost all farmers today have more than one source of income."[42] Logsdon reminds the reader many times that even today's large, industrial farms require federal subsidies. He goes over in considerable, practical detail, the ins and outs of input costs, land costs, financing costs, soil fertility, yield, taste, food quality, and quality of life. He hails the virtues of "stay small and stay in," his response to former Agriculture Secretary Earl Butz's famous admonition to farmers, "Get big or get out." Logsdon isn't afraid to go really small, while thinking really big:

> And while I'm talking crazy, what if there were a hundred million people in the United States raising a half-acre of corn as a hobby? That would add up to enough corn for all our food needs and no one would make monetary profit doing it [...] And wouldn't it make at least as much economic sense as maybe a couple hundred thousand farmers spending billions to grow corn and still having to be kept afloat by government subsidies and borrowed money?[43]

Such provocative musing provides a broad framework. It readies us to realize that the Golden Mean is elusive, yet again, when it comes to investing. As elusive as the questions: How much return is enough to compensate for how much risk? How does the risk an investor suffers compare to the risk a farmer takes? Is there something qualitatively different about providing financial support to a farmer? What about a local baker?

We're going to need a new kind of investing. Or, a new kind of philanthropy. Or, a new hybrid of the two.

* * * * *

Philanthropy 1.0: Become a captain of industry and make as much money as possible, so you will have more to give away.

Philanthropy 2.0: Create a private foundation and give away more than the IRS mandated 5%; or, if you are a billionaire, sign the Buffett-Gates Giving Pledge, committing to give away at least 50% of your fortune while you are still alive.

Philanthropy 3.14 (named in honor of π, the ultimately mysterious, apparently infinite irrational number that is essential in quantifying that most perfect manifestation of non-linearity that never appears perfectly in nature, the circle): Invest charitably, locally, directly, return-agnostically, and slowly in small businesses that are vital to the health of household, community, bioregion, and soil.

* * * * *

We are all earthworms. The modern economy is a plow. We have been displaced. Some will create myths that tell us we don't any longer need the soil. Some will lobby for anti-deracination tax policy.[44] Some will invent Survival Apparatus and Other Essential Tools for Uber-Terrestrial Living and Exploration. Some venturesome annelids with a good sense of rhythm and decent singing voices will write ballads about casting their fate to the wind. Some will do what they can to return.

44   Deracination is "the act of uprooting " or "displacement from one's native environment."

* * * * *

This is where compost comes in.

Composting is, perhaps, the purest, humblest, most direct manifestation of returning, putting back into the soil what we take out, prompting us to question where the world of financial return starts and the world of Sir Albert Howard's Law of Return

45   Over the years, Eliot has taken delivery, at
      Four Season Farm, Harborside, Maine, of horse
      manure, on occasion, for roughly $20/yard.

46   "You know that sharp odor of chlorine from the
      swimming pool you can recall from earliest
      childhood? It turns out it's not just chlorine, but
      a potent brew of chemicals that form when
      chlorine meets sweat, body oils, and urine. But
      up until now, just how much urine has been
      difficult to measure, says chemist Xing-Fang Li of
      the University of Alberta. Li and her colleagues
      report they can now tell roughly how much pee is
      in a pool by measuring the artificial sweeteners
      carried in most people's urine. Certain sweeten-
      ers can be a good proxy for pee, she says, because
      they're designed to 'go right through you' and
      don't break down readily in pool water. The
      scientists calculated that one 220,000 gallon,
      commercial-size swimming pool contained
      almost 20 gallons of urine. In a residential
      pool (20 by 40 foot, five feet deep), that would
      translate to about two gallons of pee. It's only
      about one-hundredth of a percent, but any urine
      in a swimming pool can be a health concern for
      some people, not to mention that smell that
      never quite goes away." (*Just How Much Pee Is In
      That Pool?* Erika Engelhaupt, NPR, March 1, 2017)

ends. If Escher's work is an ultra-sophisticated, visual primal scream, composting is a gentle, insistent, terrestrial whisper.

Consider the relationship between composting and the economy.

Composting done on-farm or at home is an exercise in creating value outside the money economy. It does very little to grow GDP. It uses natural processes of decay, decomposition, and recycling to reduce the need to purchase fertilizer. It promotes the growth of soil microbial populations, contributing to plant vigor and reducing the need for chemical control of pathogens. It keeps food and yard waste out of commercial waste treatment systems.

Now, for the home composter, there are certainly purchases that may be made, such as manufactured compost bins or tumblers, or commercially prepared bacterial inoculants to supercharge the compost pile. That's a bit of economic activity. And for composting on a small farm, there is some equipment and labor devoted to hauling in various free compost ingredients, for example, seaweed and crab shells and unwanted hay cuttings from neighboring fields, if you are Eliot Coleman.[45] Still, you are talking about precious little economic activity.

Send your food waste and yard scraps into the industrial composting system, however, and you join the economy in more significant ways. About 30 million tons of food waste goes into American landfills annually; hundreds of thousands of tons are currently diverted by commercial composting operations, feeding a $3 billion municipal composting industry. In Boulder County, Colorado, 26,000 tons per year of food waste and yard scraps are collected for composting. You can buy a 1.5 cubic foot bag of locally sourced compost, produced by Western Disposal, at Harlequin's Gardens in North Boulder, for $6.

As with GDP, we must ask, at some point, mustn't we: *What's in it?* Is the output of industrial-scale composting clean humus? It looks like nice, dark soil. But to what extent is it humus-like, manufactured-soil-ish product? How clean was the feedstock? What about microscopic remnants of plastic and food packaging? Food processing additives? Any Stay Puft Marshmallow in there? Does it contain residues of Roundup from yard waste? Other chemicals used in lawn and garden care? How is it as a microbial habitat? *What's in it?!*

These questions arise in the shadow of Jumbo Goddamn Mumbo's Law of Surreptitious Garbage Disposal and Urination, which states: Throwing questionable substances into the curbside compost collection receptacle is as inevitable as peeing in a swimming pool, only not as satisfying.[46]

(Keep in mind that there is a whole other discussion to be had about the treatment of sewage and the composting of human waste.)[47]

It might not be too much of a stretch to suggest that if GDP is the figure, then compost is the ground—the actual ground, the soil, but also actions that promote health outside the money economy.

* * * * *

The relationship of composting to the money economy reminds me of a thought experiment that I learned from my friend Alan AtKisson, a sustainability consultant who works with communities and corporations around the world.

"How many people walked here today?" he asked at a public meeting. A few hands went up.

"If you walked here, you did almost nothing for the economy. You wore down the soles of your shoes a bit, and eventually you'll need to repair or replace them, but that's about it in terms of your contribution to the economy. You also got an aerobic workout, which improved your health and might have reduced some of your health care costs in the long term, so maybe your contribution to the economy was negative."

"How many people rode a bicycle to get here?" A few more hands went up.

"You did a little something for the economy. Your bike had to be purchased. It has to be maintained. You wore down your tires a bit. Maybe you even had a flat. So, you contributed to the economy more than those who walked."

"How many people rode mass transit?" A few hands went up. "If you rode mass transit, you're starting to be involved in some real economic activity. Buses and subways are expensive to manufacture, maintain, and insure. Drivers have to be paid."

"OK, how many of you drove here?" The vast majority of hands went up. "You are economic heroes! You spend thousands of dollars a year on your car—purchasing or leasing, maintaining, fueling, insuring. You are economic heroes."

A few people chuckled, beginning to sense the disconnect between economic heroism and so many other things that matter, but then he asked, almost as an afterthought, "Wait a minute. Did anyone happen to have an accident while they were driving here?" Scattered chuckles turned into a more general murmur. "If you'd

47   One of my favorite opening lines is from *The Humanure Handbook*, a minor classic self-published by Joseph Jenkins, of Grove City, Pennsylvania: "The world is divided into two categories of people: those who shit in drinking water and those who don't." So, in Jenkins' honor, I'd like to take a shot at making this footnote one of my personal favorites. If the following text were screened, turned, sorted, and otherwise properly tended, it might turn into a handful of well-crafted paragraphs; as it is, however, you will have to deal with it as an undifferentiated heap, a compost pile that hasn't heated up. I'll number a series of items, but they aren't sequential, and should be treated as curiosities, rather than markers. *First*, there is Abby Rockefeller's paper, "Civilization and Sludge." You can pretty much tell where it is going from the title. She decries the sludge that is created by municipal sewage treatment as, "the quintessential example of disparate matter lost to use through unresolvable homogenization." We are presented with a kind of anti-Humpty Dumpty problem: Everything that comes from toilets and drains, private and commercial, is "put together again" in a toxic slew, the disposal of which presents a major systemic problem. The EPA describes the ingredients of sludge as follows: "The chemical composition and biological constituents of the sludge depend upon the composition of the wastewater entering the treatment facilities and the subsequent treatment processes. Typically, these constituents may include volatiles, organic solids, nutrients, disease-causing pathogenic organisms (e.g., bacteria, viruses, etc.), heavy metals and inorganic ions, and toxic organic chemicals from industrial wastes, household chemicals, and pesticides." Not sure why this description didn't specifically mention pharmaceuticals, fertilizers, and herbicides, although the categories *industrial wastes* and *household chemicals* do cover a lot of territory. *Second*, Jenkins' book is a wildly humanistic, hippie-ish, humble, humorous, practical exploration of everything you never wanted to know about excrement, the history of the flush toilet, the profligate use of clean water to transport raw human waste, problems caused by human manure not being understood as a vital ingredient in the cycle of maintaining soil organic matter and the sustainable production of food, the design and use of composting toilets

— Continued in margin of following page —

and other methods of handling *humanure*, and the science of composting, that is, what happens chemically and biologically in a compost pile in terms of heating up, killing pathogens, and promoting healthy microbial activity. Jenkins concludes, "Pollution from sewage and synthetic fertilizers results in part from the belief that humanure and food refuse are waste materials rather than recyclable natural resources. There is, however, an alternative. Humanure and food refuse can be composted and therefore rendered hygienically safe for agricultural or garden use. Much of the Eastern world recycles humanure. Those parts of the world have known for millennia that humanure is a valuable resource which should be returned to the land, as any animal manure should. The West has yet to arrive at that conclusion." *Third*, imagine Abby Rockefeller inviting Carlo Petrini into her basement, where she opens the mouldering compartment of her Clivus Multrum composting toilet and scoops out, for all to admire, the cured compost. (It happened. I was lucky enough to be there.) *Fourth*, such talk isn't New Age, it's Old World. Older than Old World. In *Farmers of Forty Centuries*, Dr. F.H. King, a former chief of the Division of Soil Management of the U.S. Department of Agriculture, examined how farmers in Japan, Korea, and China farmed the same fields for 4,000 years without destroying soil fertility. His book, published in 1910, reported "the most remarkable agricultural practices of well-nigh universal conservation and utilization of human waste [...] turning it to marvelous account in the maintenance of soil fertility and the production of food." Given the prominence of that part of the world in today's news (most recently with respect to North Korea's nuclear program), let's stick a little bit longer with King's observations of Far Eastern agriculture more than a century ago: "In China, in Korea, and in Japan all but the inaccessible portions of their vast extent of mountain and hill lands have long been taxed to their full capacity for fuel, lumber, and herbage for green manure and compost material; and the ash of practically all the fuel and of all of the lumber used at home finds its way ultimately to the fields as fertilizer. In China, enormous quantities of canal mud are applied to the fields, sometimes at the rate of even 70 and more tons per acre. So, too, where there are no canals, both soil and subsoil are carried into the villages and there between the intervals when needed they are,

— *Continued in margin of opposite page* —

48   *The Little Big Number: How GDP Came to Rule the World and What to Do About It*, Dirk Philipsen (Princeton University Press, 2015) p. 262

gotten into an accident, a really serious one, and an ambulance had taken you to the hospital, and you went into a coma and then were in intensive care for days, and when you came out, you had a mid-life crisis and divorced your wife and your whole family went into therapy—then you'd be an economic superhero!"

* * * * *

Consider the following description of shoe manufacturing as another example of the disconnect between economic growth and social and environmental health:

> If we were to trace the journey of an average shoe from production to consumption—materials that go into the shoe, workers traveling to the shoe factory, packaging for the shoe, shipping from production to warehouses to place of sale—we arrive at a distance that would allow us to travel around the entire globe twice, for each pair of shoes. Originally, shoes were locally produced with natural materials that were biodegradable at the end of the shoe's lifetime. No longer. Modern shoes are full of toxins—chromium, lead, plastics—which eventually degrade as pollution into the atmosphere and soil.

> We are used to buying shoes that last no more than a year or two. All the energy and resources that went into the shoes' production and sale end up, in short order, at the dump. Of course, in our economy, that's the whole point—both planned and perceived obsolescence promote growth of GDP: the faster a product becomes waste, the better. And since most of us would rather pay $90 for a pair of shoes that last a year than pay $300 for a pair that last ten, local shoe manufacturers in places from Athens or Berlin to Sydney and Washington have all but disappeared. Local communities are the poorer for it.

> This is what we call progress: workers who have been displaced from the land that used to sustain them, often in large-scale efforts to generate the raw materials necessary to manufacture things like shoes, are working long hours under deplorable working conditions. They produce cheap shoes for the ever-changing tastes of a mass market thousands of miles away consisting of people most of whom have long lost decent production jobs to lower-wage competitors in developing nations. To make this all work, we use up huge amounts of nonrenewable energy and raw materials and annually create mountains of discarded shoe piles.

> It is a problem that requires both local and global solutions.[48]

Now, before you throw this little exegesis on shoe manufacturing out with the bathwater, I'll just say that I have not independently fact checked the assertion that the making of a pair of shoes requires, in terms of total transportation of materials and people, the equivalent of two global circumnavigations; I did, however, check Philipsen's citation, which refers to a very widely respected book, *Cradle to Cradle*, by Braungart and McDonough. (The abundance of citations in Philipsen's book makes me look like a piker. Seventy-two pages containing 730 footnotes at the back of his book, along with a 36-page bibliography, are almost as chockful of life as a trowel of soil.) Even if Philipsen's description of shoe workers displaced from the land rings a bit too Marxian to your ears, and Braungart and McDonough were only as right as Malthus in terms of the specifics of their arithmetic, the larger point—the impulse to look beyond GDP, to acknowledge the severity of its *groundlessness*—remains.

Let's ask: How many and what kind of shoes would we buy if they had to end up in our own compost pile and, thence, in our kitchen garden?

* * * * *

Which brings us back, by playful swerve of organic inquiry and exploratory recirculation, to the subject of carbon.

Most of us now know that too much of it in the atmosphere is a problem. Fewer of us know that too little of it in the soil is a problem. Even fewer of us know that a significant source of atmospheric carbon is something that we've grown up thinking is as American as amber waves of grain. That something is agriculture, generally, and plowing, in particular.

"Yes, you read that correctly," writes David Mongtomery in *Growing a Revolution: Bringing Our Soil Back to Life*. "The plow. That iconic symbol of our agricultural roots that helped launch civilization as we know it. The plow enabled few to feed many and set the table for the rise of commerce, city-states, and hierarchical societies with priests, princes, politicians, and all the rest of us who don't farm. The problem, in a nutshell, is that the plow makes land vulnerable to erosion by wind and rain."

When you look at the plow from the top down, from the perspective of a farmer seeking faster ways to incorporate amendments into the soil, speed up soil oxygenation, and control weeds, it looks one way. It looks very different when you consider it from the bottom up—from the perspective of soil organic matter, conditions conducive to life in the soil, and carbon sequestration.

at the expense of great labor, composted with organic refuse and often afterwards dried and pulverized before being carried back and used on the fields as home-made fertilizers. Manure of all kinds, human and animal, is religiously saved and applied to the fields in a manner which secures an efficiency far above our own practices. Statistics obtained through the Bureau of Agriculture, Japan, place the amount of human waste in that country in 1908 at 23,950,295 tons, or 1.75 tons per acre of her cultivated land. The International Concession of the city Shanghai, in 1908, sold to a Chinese contractor the privilege of entering residences and public places early in the morning of each day in the year and removing the night soil, receiving therefor more than $31,000, gold, for 78,000 tons of waste. All of this we not only throw away but expend much larger sums in doing so." *Fifth*, Sir Francis Bacon opined, in 1625, "Money is like muck. Not good, except it be spread."

4 PER 1000

CARBON SEQUESTRATION IN SOILS
FOR FOOD SECURITY AND THE CLIMATE

Ministère de l'Agriculture, de l'Agroalimentaire et de la Forêt

The quantity of carbon contained in the **atmosphere** increases by **4.3 billion tons** every year

+4.3 bn tons carbon / year

↑↑

CO₂ emissions

Forests ⊖⊖
Oceans ⊖⊖
Human activities ⊕⊕⊕⊕
Deforestation ⊕

⊖ absorption ⊕ emission

The world's **soils** contain **1 500 billion tons** of carbon in the form of organic material

absorption of CO₂ by plants

↓↓

↓↓

storage of organic carbon in soils

1 500 bn tons carbon

If we increase by **4‰** (0.4%) a year the quantity of carbon contained in soils, **we can halt the annual increase in CO₂ in the atmosphere,** which is a major contributor to the greenhouse effect and climate change

increased absorption of CO₂ by plants :

↓↓

farmlands, meadows, forests…

↓↓ **+4‰** carbon storage in the world's soils

= more fertile soils
= soils better able to cope with the effects of climate change

HOW CAN SOILS STORE MORE CARBON?

The more soil is covered, the richer it will be in organic material and therefore in carbon.
Until now, the combat against global warming has largely focused on the protection and restoration of forests.
In addition to forests, we must encourage more plant cover in all its forms.

Never leave soil bare and work it less, for example by using no-till methods

Introduce more intermediate crops, more row intercropping and more grass strips

Add to the hedges at field boundaries and develop agroforestry

Optimize pasture management – with longer grazing periods, for example

Restore land in poor condition e.g. the world's arid and semi-arid regions

*"This international initiative can reconcile the aims of **food security** and the **combat against climate change,** and therefore engage every concerned country in COP21."*

Stéphane Le Foll, French Minister of Agriculture, Agrifood and Forestry

Rattan Lal, a widely respected soil scientist at The Ohio State University, estimates that since the beginning of the Industrial Revolution, more than a quarter of all carbon added to the atmosphere has come from plowing, which speeds up decomposition of soil organic matter and exposes soil to wind and rain, thereby increasing erosion. According to Lal's estimates, between 66 billion and 90 billion tons of soil carbon has been lost, representing as much as half of all original soil carbon. Today, 15–20% of total annual greenhouse gas emissions are attributed to agriculture, much of that from plowing.

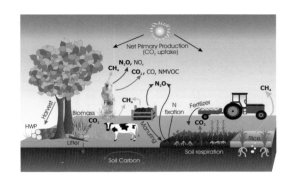

The good news is that carbon can be put back into the soil by no-till farming practices, the application of compost and manure, and the holistic grazing of livestock.

There are all manner of studies and groups working on this. Rodale Institute has been conducting no-till farming trials for decades, leading the way on empirical demonstrations of the role of soil organic matter. The Savory Institute and its pioneering founder, Allan Savory, have also been leading the way, in this case, focused on livestock and the ability of intensive rotational grazing and holistic management to counter desertification and promote large-scale grassland restoration and carbon sequestration. Soil4Climate and The Carbon Underground advocate for soil restoration as a climate solution. The Carbon Cycle Institute's report "Healthy Soils, Healthy Communities" documents community-scale work being done in California to build soil carbon. The Marin Carbon Project finds that a single layer of compost less than an inch thick applied to the surface of pasture stimulates microbial and plant activity, resulting in the sequestration of 1.5 tons of carbon per acre on a continual basis. The French National Institute for Agricultural Research announced, in the run up to the 2015 UN Climate Change Conference, a "4 per 1000" initiative, aimed at building soil organic matter .4% per annum. (See opposite page.)

Michael Pollan, one of the world's leading proponents of healthy food systems and healthy agriculture, writes:

> Some scientists project that 75 to 100 parts per million of CO_2 could be drawn out of the atmosphere over the next century if existing farms, pastures and forestry systems were managed to maximize carbon sequestration. That's significant when you consider that CO_2 levels passed 400 ppm this spring. Scientists agree that the safe level of carbon dioxide in the atmosphere is 350 ppm.
>
> Regenerative farming would also increase the fertility of the land, making it more productive and better able to absorb and hold water, a critical function

especially in times of climate-related floods and droughts. Carbon-rich fields require less synthetic nitrogen fertilizer and generate more productive crops, cutting farmer expenses.[49]

Yet is there anything more charged, in the current political climate, than citing scientists? This is one climate in which change would not be a bad thing—not change with respect to political party or politician, but change with respect to tenor, rancor, and distrust.

If a senior scientist at the Pesticide Action Network states that for every 8.4 tons of carbon sequestered per acre, the ability to hold water increases by 25,000 gallons, should I believe her?[50] I do, but I'm not asking you to. I'm asking you to believe your eyes and ears and trust your common sense.

I first saw the accompanying photo (see margin) at a conference presentation by Jeff Moyer, of the Rodale Institute, ten years ago. The jar on the right contains a clod of earth that is low in organic matter so, rather than holding water, it easily dissolves and is subject to erosion. The jar on the left is a clod rich in carbon, so it holds water and maintains its coherence and integrity.

I offer for your consideration, therefore, another proposition, hoping to bring science down to earth, minimizing the potential for rancor and distrust:

COHERENCE AND INTEGRITY, GOOD; EROSION, BAD.

* * * * *

If we can learn to see science in ways that are pragmatic, can we also learn to see finance in ways that are poetic? The following insights of renowned conservationist Aldo Leopold describe a fund in a way no financier ever has:

> Land, then, is not merely soil: it is a fountain of energy flowing through a circuit of soils, plants and animals. Food chains are the living channels which conduct energy upward; death and decay return it to the soil. The circuit is not closed; some energy is dissipated in decay, some is added by absorption from the air, some is stored in soils, peats and long-lived forests; but it is a sustained circuit, like a slowly augmented revolving fund of life.[51]

You don't have to be an angry voter or an Occupier to harbor a healthy skepticism of financial systems that govern industry and commerce with the greatest

49   "A Secret Weapon to Fight Climate Change: Dirt," Debbie Barker and Michael Pollan, *Washington Post*, December 4, 2015

50   "Carbon Farming as Climate Solution," Margaret Reeves, National Sustainable Agriculture Coalition, June 8, 2016

(Jeff Moyer/Rodale Institute)

51   *A Sand County Almanac*, Aldo Leopold (Oxford University Press, 1989) p. 216

computational sophistication, yet cannot reconcile themselves with the most basic aspects of nature and its underlying poetry.

* * * * *

Earthworms. Microbes. Compound interest. Moore's Law. A reporter seeking ways to have your cake while making 7%. Numbers vs. words. M.C. Escher. GDP. Bhutan. Composting. Toxic shoes. Carbon farming.

We need to add two more spices to our meta-economic, sub-soil recipe: *flow* and *flerds*.

I first heard about glomalin from Joan Gussow, pioneer of nutritional ecology and beloved thought leader of the local food movement: "Glomalin, which literally holds our soils together, was considered an unidentified contaminant of humus until 1996. A contaminant! Think how lucky we are that we never got around to eliminating it!" Glomalin is a sticky protein that plays a key role facilitating bidirectional flow—nutrients flowing from soil to plant roots and dissolved carbon, from photosynthesis, flowing from plant roots to the soil. Glomalin coats filaments of mycorrhizal fungi, enabling this flow. Eventually, glomalin-coated filaments detach into the soil, where they perform a glue-like function, binding to sand, silt, and clay particles, forming aggregates that give soil its tilth—the porosity and stability that are key to the flow of water and nutrients, the infiltration of oxygen, and the movement of soil denizens.

Meanwhile, above ground, on rangeland and pasture, roam the flerds. OK, just as you might suspect, there's no such thing as a flerd—except there is, in the mind and on the rangeland of one Eric Harvey, who runs cows and sheep together on his 7,000 acre farm in Australia:

> It's called a *flerd*—a flock of sheep and a herd of cattle, commingled. Years ago he had seen sheep and cattle grazing together in Africa and thought, "That makes sense." Maybe to Eric—but not to many others. To say that it is not traditional to run cows and sheep together would be a huge understatement. It's hardly done anywhere. Not only do many in agriculture consider the two types of herbivores to be incompatible with each other from a grazing perspective, but most sheep and cattle farmers consider *each other* to be incompatible as well. In fact, Australia endured its share of range wars between sheepmen and stockmen over the decades, much like America did in the nineteenth century.

Eric ignored all that, and in 2005 he put together his first flerd, eventually commingling five thousand sheep and six hundred cows. His goal was to use the different grazing behaviors of sheep and cattle to benefit plant vigor, diversity, and density. "Nature likes mixed-species grazing," Eric said, "because animals often complement each other in what they will eat, the composition of their manure, and the way their hooves interact with the soil." As Eric described it, herbivory creates an organic pulse *below* the ground surface as roots expand and contract with grazing. This feeds carbon to hungry fungi, protozoa, and nematodes, which in turn feed grass plants. The manure pulse above ground helps too, especially with nutrient cycling. His plan with the flerd was to make both pulses beat stronger and more steadily.[52]

52   *Grass, Soil, Hope: A Journey Through Carbon Country,*
      Courtney White (Chelsea Green, 2014) pp. 80-81

Pulse, cycle, bidirectional flow, diversity, interdependence, plants and animals, biology and chemistry, sheep and cattle, working together, above ground and below—such is the stuff of soil fertility and soil carbon, and it should encourage us, with an irrational exuberance of the symbiotic kind, to consider a whole new spin on the concept of return.

* * * * *

The nurture capitalist writes in his notebook:

> *Impoverished is the culture that chases industrial efficiency and technological disruption, as if there were no return.*
>
> *Poor is the soil from which much is taken and little returned.*
>
> *No financial return, no metric, no matter how faithfully computed, will reconnect us to one another, to the places where we live and to the land.*
>
> *Financial return is a poor man's compass.*

* * * * *

In the end, of course, when it comes to something as nuanced as the interactions between economy, ecology, and culture, we have more questions than answers.

What happens when the Law of Return meets financial rate of return? Can soil fertility be translated into an asset class that delivers predictable investment returns? If Sir Albert Howard broke bread with Jeremy Grantham, Joan Gussow, and Nell Newman, what kind of investment scheme would they devise?

A Mastercard TV commercial might offer a quasi-answer, "Soil fertility? Priceless." But we don't actually live in a Mastercard commercial (although it sometimes does feel that way). We are left with the task of determining how much of our money we are willing to invest as if food, farms, and fertility mattered. *Are we going to get our money back? Are we going to make a little money? What if we lose some money but end up with thousands of acres of beautiful, productive, carbon-sequestering, nutritious food-producing soil in our community, under the stewardship of scores of farmers and hundreds of workers and a bunch of related small food enterprises? What if we made 0% loans in pursuit of this end, leaving our financial returns in, sequestering them, for the benefit of all?*

III   Nurture

That's just what a few of us have set out to do in Colorado. We're putting some of our money back into the soil, leaving the returns in.

We call it SOIL: Slow Opportunities for Investing Locally. SOIL is pooling donations, and then, by majority vote of those who donate—one person, one vote, no matter what the size of the donation—making 0% loans to local farmers and small food entrepreneurs. (More on this project is presented in Section IV.)

This is slow money at work in one community, but it is embedded in a larger context. I think of that context as an emerging field called *nurture capital*. When the term nurture capital first suggested itself, I thought it was intriguing, an interesting talking point, but not *real*. I've begun to think differently over the past few years. (Not about the intriguing part.)

America has *venture capital*—tens of billions of dollars a year going to high tech, capital intensive start-ups. We have *philanthropy*—tens of billions a year going to non-profits from private foundations and hundreds of billions of dollars a year going from individuals to churches, schools, hospitals, community foundations, poverty programs, disaster relief, the arts, and the environment.[1] What is missing? *Nurture capital*—billions of dollars a year from local individuals to businesses that are preserving and restoring the health of the land and the community.

Community development financial institutions, credit unions, microfinance, the Small Business Administration, and crowdfunding work to improve access to capital, democratize finance, or improve economic prospects for disadvantaged segments of the population. The U.S. Department of Agriculture, Farm Bureau, Sustainable Agriculture and Food Systems Funders Group (a coalition of 100 funders, mostly foundations), American Farmland Trust, and an emerging cohort of private impact funds provide funding and technical assistance for young farmers, farmland investment, conservation easements, rural development, and agricultural technologies. The latter category also attracts some venture capital. These are all vital, but we need more. We need to imagine, and then create, new ways for capital to flow, organized not only around the money, but also around what some call *social capital*.[2] Can money, the very stuff of transactions, be used in new ways that foster

[1] While 2015 was the most charitable year on record, with total giving by individuals and foundations of $373 billion, the category Environment/Animals was flat as a percentage of the total, coming in at less than 4%. In descending order, giving went to Religion, Education, Human Services, Foundations, Health, Public-Society Benefit, Arts/Culture/Humanities, International Affairs, and Environment/Animals. (Giving USA)

[2] We should exercise caution when using such terminology as *social capital* and *ecological capital*, terms commonly used in discussions of the triple bottom line (financial capital, social capital, ecological capital). These terms contain within them a reductionism that monetizes relationships, implying that if we get good enough at doing multi-level arithmetic calculations, values and virtue will be accounted for.

healthy relationships? Can nurture capital promote neighborliness, conviviality, civility, and fertility?

In *It All Turns on Affection*, Wendell Berry educes a deep concept of affection, extending it from an emotion shared among individuals to a sensibility that connects people to the places where they live. This kind of affection is a cultural virtue. It contributes to our sense of self-worth and belonging, our sense of purpose and dignity. Capital flowing from financial institutions and professionally managed funds tends to come at the expense of this kind of affection. This is not an inverse relationship, but it is a delicate one. Places are susceptible to the untoward influences of markets, just as quality is susceptible to the untoward influences of quantity.

Our affection and our sense of place are threatened not only by distant markets, but also by urbanization. Uncharted geographical frontiers used to beckon those in search of freedom and opportunity; today, it is cities. I once read in the book review of a Middle Eastern author something to the effect that "all the young men are leaving the villages and moving to the city, to drink Coca-Cola and watch Brigitte Bardot movies." We accept this as inevitable. And it has been, over the past century.

On May 23, 2007, the world officially became more urban than rural. The global proportion of urban population rose from 13% (220 million) in 1900, to 29% (732 million) in 1950, to 50% (3.3 billion) in 2007. Today, 54% of the world population is urban, expected to increase to 66%, or 6 billion people, by 2050. In urbanization, the U.S. has been exceptional. The U.S. became more urban than rural roughly a hundred years ago. 85% of Americans are urban, today. Paralleling urbanization has been the industrialization of agriculture.

Shall we imagine that this process is destined to continue in a straight line? Leading where? To a few dozen American farms, tens of millions of acres each, managed by fleets of drones and combines the size of aircraft carriers, producing enormous quantities of a handful of agricultural commodities as ingredients for manufactured food products that are engineered to appear varied, but are woefully deficient in biodiversity? Or, as surely as what goes east eventually ends up west, will balance be found somewhere between here and there? Perhaps even a little bit back from where we are today?

Ahh, the Luddite hecklers are gathering to enjoy their heckling…

* * * * *

If I were to say, "I am not a Luddite," I'd hear echoes of President Nixon saying, "I am not a crook." But really, I am not a Luddite.

I do have Luddite sympathies, however, and I'm not sure why that would be considered a negative, except by the most hardened apologists for all things industrial, mercantile, and fiduciary. After all, the Luddites were objecting to Dickensian working conditions in the English mills and the displacement of peasants from the countryside and the commons. The destructive part of Schumpeter's creative destruction was in full force in those early days of the Industrial Revolution—it still is today, and in accelerated form.[3] Violent pushback against such displacement lands with a thud in the two wrongs don't make a right department, but that doesn't mean our sympathies should be stunted. I'm sure I'll get in all manner of trouble with historians, but it occurs to me that the Luddites could have been the Trump voters of their age. Their way of life and sense of self-worth were being hijacked by industrialization, urbanization, and globalization. So, historians and Luddite hecklers, have at it.[4]

I do have Luddite sympathies. When I consume industrial products, I wonder about the conditions in which they were produced, about mountains of discarded electronics being sifted through in India, and about five trillion pieces of plastic in the ocean (that is, almost a thousand pieces of floating plastic ocean debris for every person on the planet, with no end in sight). I am unsettled by the prospect of hundreds of millions of Chinese peasants migrating to cities. And by the use of the term *farms* to describe warehouses full of computer servers springing up in America's heartland.[4]

I wonder and I am unsettled, but I still consume. Guilt and befuddlement are often lurking. Yet, I enjoy my new MacBook as much as the next person.

Then I migrate, in thought and in action, towards the possibilities of nurture capital.

* * * * *

Just as to a hammer everything looks like a nail, to Wall Street every promising commercial venture looks like a corporate, financially-engineered pot of gold at the end of a large, public-market rainbow. These attitudes cast a long shadow. We start to believe that the only measures of success are market size, profitability, scalability, and capital gain. This thinking elbows the pursuit of long-term health so far into the background that it virtually disappears.

3 "Industrial mutation—if I may use the biological term— [...] incessantly revolutionizes the economic structure *from within*, incessantly destroying the old one, incessantly creating a new one. This process of Creative Destruction is the essential fact about capitalism." Joseph Schumpeter, *Capitalism, Socialism and Democracy* (Harper & Row, New York, 1975) p. 83

4 KANSAS CITY, MO. - "A new kind of farm is popping up. Tucked away on small plots on America's back roads, it cultivates no soil or seed. Rather, it nurtures curiosities about everything from porn to pinochle expressed in a nearly endless sequence of 1s and 0s queried from desktops, laptops, and iPhones around the globe. The computer server farm—huge banks of computer servers doing the heavy-lifting logic of Internet giants like Google, Yahoo, and Amazon—is bringing bits of Silicon Valley to places like Pryor, Oklahoma, and Council Bluffs, Iowa [...] Server farms also guzzle electricity, the way computer technicians gulp Red Bull. The farms are massive, up to football-field-sized buildings filled with racks of servers [...] Server farms can grow huge, consuming up to 100 megawatts of electricity [...] Server farms, like their agricultural counterparts, require ever fewer people to produce even more. The facility going up in Council Bluffs will need only 100 workers to tend to thousands of computers that represent a $300 million investment by the company. And it plans to double the facility. 'It's big,' said Mark Norman of the Council Bluffs Area Chamber of Commerce. 'And it's only getting bigger.'" Sam Savage, *Server Farms Become a Cash Crop in the Midwest*, May 7, 2008 (redOrbit.com)

At the end of the economic rainbow for a small, local, organic food enterprise is not an Initial Public Offering, but an actual rainbow over carbon-rich fields of organic vegetables and pasture-raised livestock. Looked at from global markets down, it is difficult to take these businesses seriously. Looked at from systemic social and environmental problems down, small local food investments, and gaggles of local investors who make them, don't seem effectual. Looked at from enormous pools of capital down, small and mid-size farms, CSAs, farmers markets, heirloom seed companies, composting businesses, and local food processors and distributors don't compute.

Looked at from the ground up, however, the value of all these can be seen. Yet, considerable ambiguity remains. *How small is small? How local is local? How slow is slow? Can we actually build profitable investment portfolios supporting the next generation of soil tenders?* These aren't exactly zen koans, but neither are they questions which need to be answered with precision. It is in the very way they enable us to hold qualitative judgments coequal with economic metrics that their value lies.

* * * * *

The case for a radical rebalancing of quality and quantity is made as well as any human can make it by Wendell Berry in *The Unsettling of America*, a copy of which has never been far from my desk for the past 40 years. (Those who know me may be joining at this moment in an exercise of collective eye-rolling that rivals that of *Wall Street Journal* readers at the mention of Thomas Malthus. *Oh, dear, not again...* But this is another of those times when we have to return to the words.)

In fact, I keep in my travel bag the following passage from Berry's seminal volume— RFK's words about GNP on one side, these of Wendell on the other.[5] It is dog-eared, this sheet of paper, as I frequently read from it when speaking in public:

5   *The Unsettling of America*, Wendell Berry (Sierra Club Books, 1978) pp. 7–8

"I conceive a strip miner to be a model exploiter, and as a model nurturer I take the old-fashioned idea or ideal of a farmer. The exploiter is a specialist, an expert; the nurturer is not. The standard of the exploiter is efficiency; the standard of the nurturer is care. The exploiter's goal is money, profit; the nurturer's goal is health—his land's health, his own, his family's, his community's, his country's. Whereas the exploiter asks of a piece of land only how much and how quickly it can be made to produce, the nurturer asks a question that is much more complex and difficult: What is its carrying capacity? (That is, how much can be taken from it without diminishing it? What can it produce *dependably* for an indefinite time?) The exploiter wishes to earn as much as possible by as little work as possible; the nurturer expects, certainly, to have a decent living from his work, but his characteristic wish is to work as *well* as possible. The competence of the exploiter is in organization; that of the nurturer is in order--a human order, that is, that accommodates itself both to other order and to mystery. The exploiter typically serves an institution or organization; the nurturer serves land, household, community, place. The exploiter thinks in terms of numbers, quantities, hard facts; the nurturer in terms of character, condition, quality, kind."

--Wendell Berry

This is more than a remarkably coherent passage about the tension between quality and quantity, industrial and agrarian. It is the organizing vision for a whole new financial sector—nurture capital. At least, that's what I hear.

* * * * *

In taking Wendell to heart, and wishing to translate this wisdom into action, the budding nurture capitalist must avoid quantitative traps. Like the Lieber Trap—the "we want to avoid investing in this and that, we are passionately worried about this and that, but we still need our retirement account to yield 7%" trap. Which is related to the venture capitalist's 20% internal rate of return trap. Which is related to the "you can't manage what you can't measure" trap. Which is related to the Efficient Market Hypothesis trap. (Which is part and parcel of the GDP trap, but, then, you already knew that.)

That said, there are many reports by leading fiduciaries and professional analysts that can help us reckon our place in the broader scheme of things.

In May of this year, friends at Trillium Asset Management brought to our attention a new report, *Impact Investing in Sustainable Food and Agriculture Across Asset Classes: Financing Resilient Value Chains Through Total Portfolio Activation*. The report, authored by the Croatan Institute with participation from a number of leaders in food and finance, provides a broad investment framework for sophisticated and institutional investors interested in sustainable food systems. USSIF (The Forum for Sustainable and Responsible Investment) publishes a biennial report titled *U.S. Sustainable, Responsible and Impact Investing Trends*. The Wallace Global Fund's report, *Mobilizing More for Mission*, is an excellent case study of how a $150 million foundation that is addressing climate change with its grant making is also addressing the management of its investments. California Environmental Associates examines the ins and outs of investing in local food systems in their report, *Local Foods: A Guide for Investors and Philanthropists*. Related studies about funding local food systems and community food enterprises have also been published by the Springcreek Foundation and the Wallace Center at Winrock International. And on the broader question of the boundaries between philanthropy and impact investing, the Monitor Institute's *From Blueprint to Scale: The Case for Philanthropy in Impact Investing* describes a pioneer gap in funding businesses that internalize social and environmental impacts.

A few years back, the Slow Money Institute published *State of the Sector 2014*, surveying 32 investment funds, family offices, and foundations, as well as ten Slow Money investment clubs, accounting for a total of $293 million invested in 968

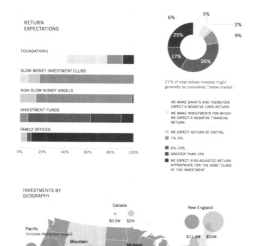

State of the Sector 2014 (Slow Money Institute)

food and agriculture deals from 2009 to 2013. The chart below illustrates where this money went:[6]

6   *State of the Sector 2014* (Slow Money Institute)

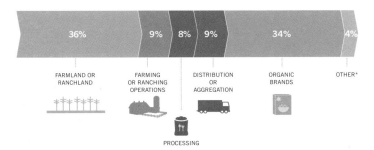

| 36% | 9% | 8% | 9% | 34% | 4% |

FARMLAND OR RANCHLAND   FARMING OR RANCHING OPERATIONS   DISTRIBUTION OR AGGREGATION   ORGANIC BRANDS   OTHER*

PROCESSING

* Farm suppliers, retail markets, urban ag, restaurants or eateries, food service/catering, co-ops, and CSAs. There is some overlap in categories (e.g., some of the farming operations may also be CSAs).

And for those who want to know how Silicon Valley approaches food and ag investment opportunities, AgFunder News tracks this world, reporting that last year venture capitalists put $4.2 billion into agtech deals, almost double the prior year, with the greatest growth in Drones/Robotics and Food Ecommerce.

This information will give the curious investor a sense of how financiers and philanthropists are looking across the boundaries and exploring food and ag.

* * * * *

Something funny happens to most professionally managed capital on its way to the soil. It gets stuck in the Other People's Money trap. (Yes, more traps.) Which is related to the brand trap. Which is related to the mouthfeel, shelf-life, product uniformity, and food technology trap. (Traps aplenty.)

I wonder if there's a Greek myth about them, these money traps. If there were, it might describe a kind of corollary to Pandora's Box. We spend centuries creating elaborate financial mechanisms to speed the flow of capital and then discover we need some slow money, but it's trapped, it can't make its way back out of all the intricate, money-accelerating machinations.

Can our money, once it has been sucked into the workings of institutional finance, zooming hither and yon in cyber this and derivative that, find its way back through all the traps, back to the soil? Trying to turn fast money into nurture capital is a little like trying to use a firehose as a drip irrigation system. No fun for either the firehose or the objects of irrigation.

Which is why the provision of nurture capital by individuals at the local level is so important.

* * * * *

The Slow Money Principles present the ethos of nurture capital. (See opposite page.)

After a discussion of these principles at a meeting in Ashland, Oregon, several years ago, an attendee said, "The innate value of this kind of investing is so obvious to me, I don't care how much money I make."

I'll never forget her words. Leaving aside the mix of prudence, enthusiasm, rashness, ignorance, knowledge, urgency, and agency in them, and the horror and derision with which they will be greeted when seeking to cross the border into the fiduciary region of the mind, the words *innate value* are laden with meaning.

If organic farms are to be factories of anything, let them be factories of innate value.

(But they really shouldn't be factories at all...)

* * * * *

Before the first page of *Animal Factory: The Looming Threat of Industrial Pig, Dairy, and Poultry Farms to Humans and the Environment*, David Kirby has placed, on a page by themselves, these two definitions:

farm \ färm\ 1. *n.*—a tract of land, usually with a house, barn, silo, etc., on which crops and often livestock are raised for livelihood

factory \ fak-t(ə-)rē \ 1. *n.*—a building or group of buildings with facilities to manufacture a uniform product, without concern for individuality

* * * * *

Perhaps the idea of nurture as an organizing principle seems naive in this age of factory farms, terrorism, and widespread political rancor. Yet, at nurture's most fundamental level—deeper than food systems, deeper than local economics, deeper, even, than the roots of perennial grasses in virgin prairie, if such a thing is possible—is an ideal that has stood the test of time, one of mankind's noblest ideals, the ideal of nonviolence.

SLOW MONEY PRINCIPLES

I We must bring money back down to earth.

II There is such a thing as money that is too fast, companies that are too big, finance that is too complex. Therefore, we must slow our money down—not all of it, of course, but enough to matter.

III The 20th Century was the era of Buy Low/Sell High and Wealth Now/Philanthropy Later—what one venture capitalist called "the largest legal accumulation of wealth in history." The 21st Century will be the era of nurture capital, built around principles of carrying capacity, care of the commons, sense of place, diversity and nonviolence.

IV We must learn to invest as if food, farms and fertility mattered. We must connect investors to the places where they live, creating healthy relationships and new sources of capital for small food enterprises.

V Let us celebrate the new generation of entrepreneurs, consumers and investors who are showing the way from Making a Killing to Making a Living.

VI Paul Newman said, "I just happen to think that in life we need to be a little like the farmer, who puts back into the soil what he takes out." Recognizing the wisdom of these words, let us begin rebuilding our economy from the ground up, asking:

— What would the world be like if we invested 50% of our assets within 50 miles of where we live?

— What if there were a new generation of companies that gave away 50% of their profits?

— What if there were 50% more organic matter in our soil 50 years from now?

If we do not take stock of our investments, in an authentic way, then our aspirations to move away from violence and towards nurture will remain half-baked.

We drive our Prii[7] to Whole Foods, while our retirement accounts are invested in Monsanto and Coca-Cola. We recycle, but trade oil stocks on our iPhones. We vote for pro-environment candidates, but don't think twice about flying whenever we can. We donate to environmental organizations, but don't know how to rid our portfolios of defense department contractors.

The American Dream is riddled with cognitive dissonance. There are American demons. We each internalize this dissonance in our own way. We each make peace between Deal Doer and Do Gooder, between objector and investor, between ideologue and neighbor, in our own way.

The peace we need to make at the political level—between red and blue, rural and urban, conservative and liberal—is obvious and much ballyhooed, although it often seems as far-fetched as politicians calling for other politicians to get beyond politics. Peace that has real roots, so that it may one day flourish and influence the realm of national politics, needs to start at a more personal, more neighborly, more earthworm-loving level.

It is not merely a footnote to history that the manufacture of fertilizer took up where the manufacture of munitions left off after WWII—ammonium nitrate is an explosive. Yet most might find it, at first blush, somewhat effete to say that industrial agriculture is waging war on soil microorganisms. Even when we apply herbicides and pesticides—chemical killing agents, some of which were used during WWII to commit genocide—it is all too easy to deny that killing weeds and insects (even when the vast majority, sometimes as much as 99% of the applied chemicals never hit the target, but go "somewhere") is a form of agricultural violence. But it is.

A production system that results in soil erosion is a form of agricultural violence. A production system that results in phosphorus run-off, algae blooms, and polluted water supplies is a form of agricultural violence. A production system that confines millions of genetically identical hogs in crates, pumps them full of antibiotics, and collects unimaginable quantities of manure in leak-prone lagoons is a form of agricultural violence. A production system that turns most of its genetically modified corn into feed for feedlots, fuel for cars, and sweeteners for junk food does harm to culture, community, and the web of life.

If the word *violence* seems too harsh, too extreme, then how about the word *immaturity*? It is hard to believe that after 10,000 years of cultivating and breeding, and

7   As voted by Toyota Prius owners in 2011, the plural of Prius is Prii. (http://toyotanews.pressroom.toyota.com/releases/toyota-announces-the-plural-of-prius.htm)

a few hundred years of industrializing, and several decades of high-technologizing, modern agriculture, and the market economy of which it is a part, could still be immature. But what else do you call a system (or a person or a nation) that is dangerously deficient in humility and self-restraint, prone to engage in destructive behavior in pursuit of short-term consumer gratification, dismissive of community, and ignorant of the fundamentals of long-term health?[8]

In the name of nonviolence, community, and health, we need to nurture greater humility and self-restraint. There is no better place to splice nurture into the genes of the economy than local food systems.

* * * * *

A few years ago, I was invited to dinner by a Slow Money supporter.

"I've told Tommy, one of my investment managers, what we are up to. I want you to meet him." Code for, "It will be entertaining to listen to you and Tommy go at it."

We had a delightful dinner—it was a beautiful summer evening at the New England shore—and then, over dessert, and after a few glasses of wine, Tommy turned to me and said, "Bill has told me a little about Slow Money. I'd like to hear it straight from the horse's mouth."

I gave him a general run down. He reflected. He sipped. And then he said, "That's preposterous. You're telling me that you want me and my partners to consider all kinds of subjective things and value judgments, things that don't have anything to do with a company's profitability or the technical criteria we use to evaluate our investments. We'd never to be able to agree. We'd never be able to make any investment decisions."

I reflected. I sipped. And then I said, "Come to think of it, that sounds good to me. I'm not worried about which investment decisions you eventually make. I just want to know that you had the arguments, that you weighed the larger concerns, then made your decisions. I think the world would be better off if investment managers did that before pulling the trigger."

We were, unfortunately, pretty much talking past one another. The scale of far-flung public ownership and the fiduciary responsibilities of companies listed on stock exchanges are as impervious to the concerns of nurture capital as macadam over bottomland.

* * * * *

8   Were the gods to ask for case studies on the violence and immaturity of the market economy, we might offer them yartsa gunbu, sometimes referred to as Tibet's golden worm. This is a story about distant, urban consumer demand colliding with rural community food tradition. Yartsa gunbu, a fungus that invades the caterpillar of the ghost moth, killing its host after it burrows a few inches into the soil, resulting in a mummified carcass with a small, above-ground protrusion, has long been prized in traditional Chinese medicine as a booster of immune response and stamina. In recent decades, spurred by its reported use by Chinese Olympic athletes and the increasing disposable income of Chinese consumers, the retail price of yartsa gunbu has increased 900%, hitting $13,000 per pound in Lhasa and double that in Shanghai. The result has been called a gold rush, with tens of thousands of seasonal foragers flooding remote provinces in China, Tibet, and Nepal, where yartsa gunbu is found at altitudes above 10,000 feet. "Recent news coverage has focused on community tensions and infighting over harvesting practices, the flood of outsiders seeking to take part in the harvest and allegations of graft and bribery among community leaders. In June 2014, a clash with police left two dead in a dispute between members of the local community and a National Park Buffer Zone Management Committee over who has the right to collect and keep fees paid by outsiders for access to yartsa gunbu grounds. Two more people died in a 2013 fight between Tibetan groups near Rebgong, China. Meanwhile, outside experts warn that over-harvest of the fungus could cause irreparable damage to fragile high-mountain pastures, with some suggesting yartsa gunbu production already had declined by 40 percent." (http://metro.co.uk/2012/09/13/what-is-yartsa-gunbu-and-why-has-it-been-dubbed-the-himalayan-viagra-573596/)

A few weeks ago, I had dinner with someone whose family office had, on his insistence, made a few investments in local organic farms. Following our dinner, I wrote him the following *Letter to a Young Nurture Capitalist.*

Dear Jeff,

At dinner last week, two things you said impelled me to put electronic pen to electronic paper.

First, you mentioned Noam Chomsky's recent observation that the obsession about Russian collusion is misplaced, particularly given U.S. interference in other countries' elections. Always good to have healthy skepticism shake up the herd mentality.

Second, you referred to your dad as a great steward of your family wealth, and your use of that word, steward, stuck with me. You said, with obvious love and respect, and, then, some resigned self-reflection, that he was a much better investor than you, given the disappointing results you've had from your first forays into investing in the local food system.

This is, of course, a subject about which I have more to say than is suitable for a note of this kind. But I wanted to flag a few things for the next time.

Using the word *steward* to describe an investor who successfully grows financial wealth is like using the word *sustainable* to describe a business, when all that is meant is that the business is a going concern, a continuing enterprise, without any of the social and environmental meanings of the term *sustainability*.

Being a good investor and being a good steward are not the same thing. A steward has to be able to keep the near-term and the long-term in focus at the same time, without becoming disoriented. An investor has an easier, more linear task, focusing on days and quarters and years, and on commercial activity, of, by and for itself. A steward does that, but also does something more complicated, taking into account the bigger picture, meaning not only on the next generation, but, with at least a little of his cognizance, the whole homo sapiens enchilada. A steward wonders, ex-plicitly and implicitly: Can we integrate our technological and commercial cleverness with our ecological and spiritual imagination, so that we can pull the ecological rabbit out of the economic hat?

You are a steward. Or, shall we say, a budding nurture capitalist. I was saddened to hear the extent to which your initial food investing has left you unsettled. One of your investments was a write-off. The other, after a few years, is not living up to your expectations. It's causing you to question the whole thing, at least as it relates to your family.

Measurable non-financial impacts are one thing, broader systemic impacts another, qualitative, cultural values and concerns another, and paying for your child's college education yet another. How can we possibly incorporate the laws of biology and ecology and gravity, the rhythms of nature, community and democracy, into the work of investing?

Which reminds me of one of my all-time favorite movie speeches, from *Network* (the 1976 movie that made famous the line: "I'm mad as hell and I'm not going to take it anymore!", but that's another scene). It's delivered by Ned Beatty, playing the CEO of a multinational that had just purchased a TV station. I've shown the clip at Slow Money events, and while I can't do justice in writing to the power of Beatty's iconic performance, I wanted to include the words of his rant:

> *You have meddled with the primal forces of nature, Mr. Beale, and I won't have it! Is that clear?!*
>
> *You think you've merely stopped a business deal. That is not the case. The Arabs have taken billions of dollars out of this country and now they must put it back! It is ebb and flow, tidal gravity. It is ecological balance! You are an old man who thinks in terms of nations and peoples. There are no nations. There are no peoples. There are no Russians. There are no Arabs. There are no Third Worlds. There is no West. There is only one holistic system of systems. One vast and immane, interwoven, interacting, multi-variant, multi-national dominion of dollars—petro-dollars, electro-dollars, multi-dollars, Reichsmarks, Yen, Rubles, Pounds and Shekels.*
>
> *It is the international system of currency which determines the totality of life on this planet.*

9   http://slowmoney.org/network-clip

That is the natural order of things today. That is the atomic, and sub-atomic, and galactic structure of things today! And you have meddled with the primal forces of nature. And you will atone!!

Am I getting through to you, Mr. Beale?

Four decades after *Network* came out, we are still dealing with the pendulum of finance and globalization. Will it ever swing back? Has it begun to swing back? Are the local food movement and organics and impact investing and B Corporations and the stock price of McDonald's the first indicators that the pendulum is going to swing back? Are we jumping onto that pendulum, doing what we can to slow it down sooner than it must otherwise?

OK. Enjoy the *Network* clip.[9]

Looking forward to our next meal.

W.

10 From 2008 to 2014, when it went public, one of the fastest growing private companies in China was Modern Dairy Holdings. Today it has 26 farms, each of which milks roughly 10,000 cows. There is no discussion on the company's website about bovine growth hormone, antibiotics, GMO corn, access to pasture, or manure management. In 2008, U.S. private equity firm KKR invested $150 million in Modern Dairy Holdings, at a time when China's milk industry was battered by a scandal involving melamine contamination. In 2011, the company touted a 26% increase in milk yield (this might mean *per cow*, but wasn't specified in the press release) via improved nutrition, breeding, and reduced disease rate. By 2013, the value of KKR's investment had tripled. (Come on, someone say it—say the words *cash cow*.)

11 According to Bill Mollison, the father of permaculture (for "permanent agriculture"): "Permaculture is a philosophy of working with, rather than against nature; of protracted and thoughtful observation, rather than protracted and thoughtless labor; and of looking at plants and animals in all their functions, rather than treating any area as a single product system." Here's another definition: "Permaculture is a creative design process based on whole-systems thinking informed by ethics and design principles [...] This approach guides us to mimic the patterns and relationships we can find in nature and can be applied to all aspects of human habitation, from agriculture to ecological building, from appropriate technology to education and even economics." (permacultureprinciples.com)

* * * * *

The nurture capitalist cannot pass GO without addressing the question of scale. Consider, in this regard, three yogurt companies.

The first is Chobani, whose ascendancy to more than $1 billion in sales in ten years is the stuff of *60 Minutes*. Recently, Chobani founder Hamdi Ulukaya, who was born to Kurdish shepherds in eastern Turkey (*chobani* means shepherd in Turkish), waxed enthusiastically about building the world's largest yogurt manufacturing plant—one million square feet—in Twin Falls, Idaho: "The piping in this plant would reach from here to Chicago." The plant has the capacity to process 11 million pounds of milk per day.

Where does that milk come from? The company makes clear that its milk is free of bovine growth hormone, but is not organic. One of the reasons cited is the insufficiency of organic milk supply. General principles of animal welfare are stated on the company's web site. The word "local" appears in terms of sourcing milk, along with a bucolic photo of a few cows grazing happily outside a red barn. There is no information about whether the local dairies have dozens, hundreds, or thousands of cows, or the extent to which these cows have access to pasture. (Note: the bovine digestive system is a highly-evolved system for turning grass into protein. *Why are they feeding us all that corn?* See sidenote, opposite page.)[10]

The second is Stonyfield Farm, which grew out of a non-profit rural education center into the nation's leading organic yogurt company. I was fortunate enough to make an investment in Stonyfield in the 1990s, as treasurer of the Jessie Smith Noyes Foundation. Stonyfield was at tens of millions of dollars in sales back then, en route, over three decades, to almost $400 million, its commitment to organics fundamental.

The third is Butterworks Farm, a family business that makes as much organic yogurt as it can from its 450-acre farm in northern Vermont. Butterworks imports precious few farm inputs and manages its herd of 45 Jerseys as organically, sustainably, regeneratively, and nurturingly as any farming enterprise I have had the pleasure to encounter. Over the decades, Butterworks hit its limit in terms of sales, as much as can be generated from that place, roughly $1 million a year. I'm pretty sure that Jack and Anne Lazor, the proprietors of Butterworks, don't use the term *mouthfeel*. (They don't need to. I speak from experience as a happy customer, back when I lived in their territory.)

Conventional industrial-scale dairy operation

To professional investors, a $1 million yogurt maker doesn't even appear on the radar. It's too small, too idiosyncratic, dependent on a husband and wife team (a serious no-no in venture capital circles) and there's no exit strategy—no way to scale the business in such a fashion that it becomes easy to take public or sell to a corporate acquirer. To folks who are lucky enough to live within the distribution radius of an organic yogurt maker like Butterworks, a way to use a little of their money to become more than consumers, to become gentle partners in the enterprise, helping it to flourish while remaining small and independent, takes on an entirely different hue.

Profit-maximizing investors with an interest in food look for the next Chobani. Impact investors with an interest in organics scour the landscape for the next Stonyfield. The imagination and affection of the nurture capitalist flow to Butterworks.

But those examples are in the weeds. Let's stay out of them for the moment, lest they prevent us from enjoying more permacultural possibilities.[11]

Jack Lazor and a few of the Butterworks Farm bovines

FIG. 1

FIG. 2

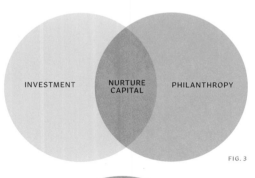

INVESTMENT NURTURE CAPITAL PHILANTHROPY

FIG. 3

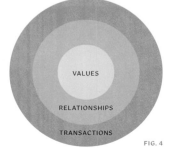

VALUES

RELATIONSHIPS

TRANSACTIONS

FIG. 4

The following thought experiment is way out of the weeds.

* * * * *

We begin with this. (FIG. 1)

We are moving towards this. (FIG. 2)

Now, let's add labels. (FIG. 3)

The work being done by so many investment managers, foundations, advisors, and innovative intermediaries in the early 21st century under the general banner of impact investing can be thought of as working from the INVESTMENT circle in and from the PHILANTHROPY circle in, with most impact investing activity occurring along the boundaries of the middle zone. The work of growing the middle zone is the work of reconnection, reintegration, healing the wounds caused by the bifurcation between private profit-making and public benefit. If you would like to imagine what those two circles might have looked like in 1900, they might have looked like Gandhi's eyeglasses, but with no bridge connecting them. (That is, two circles, with a space between them.) Then, perhaps betokening the beginning of the modern social investment movement and the advent of the anti-Apartheid campaign to divest from companies doing business in South Africa, the circles touch and begin to have a tiny overlap starting around 1970, with the area of overlap slowly increasing from then to now.

Next, let's ask, Where are we headed? What would success look like in this historic process of reconnection and healing?

It might look like this. (FIG. 4)

Think of the modern economy and efficient capital markets as the outer ring alone, TRANSACTIONS, with no inner rings—no RELATIONSHIPS or VALUES to ground them. Money zooms around faster and faster, seeking short-term profit, with no people or places or meta-economic values to ground it. Long-term health depends upon the success of efforts to put RELATIONSHIPS and VALUES into central positions, so that the power of markets may be informed, governed, disciplined, corralled, focused, amplified by, and rooted in, the stewardship of relationships and respect for cultural values.

Stated in terms of intellectual history, those same labels might be restated like this. (FIG. 5)

Here, values are expressed as BIOPHILIA—E.O. Wilson's term for the innate affection humans feel towards all other living organisms. Biophilia informs the social contract, which Adam Smith called MORAL SENTIMENTS. These then discipline the power of markets, or, to use Adam Smith's iconic phrase, the INVISIBLE HAND of the marketplace.[12]

Now, let's play some more with the labels. (FIG. 6)

We live every day in relation to these three—ECONOMY, COMMUNITY, and DIGNITY. Our first allegiance goes daily to ECONOMY. What is left over when we get home from work goes to COMMUNITY, which includes family, friends, neighbors, civic engagement, and church. What is meant by DIGNITY? It refers to what is left at our personal core—how, beyond our economic selves and our social selves, we define a clear set of personal values and a sense of our authentic self as an agent in the world. If we want to more accurately depict this, the circles might look like this. (FIG. 7)

You dig? Which brings me to my own version of dignity. *Digging.* With hands and trowel or, for the more ambitious, a walk-behind tiller. Or, for those no-tillers among us, broad fork, hoe, and other appropriate hand tools. Putting our hands in the soil.

We can also think of the three circles this way. (FIG. 8)

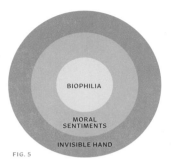

FIG. 5

FIG. 6

FIG. 7

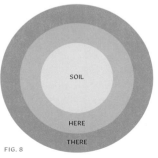

FIG. 8

12   Prior to *The Wealth of Nations*, Smith wrote *The Theory of Moral Sentiments.* Many Adam Smith scholars have noted that he never intended to suggest that the invisible hand would become the entire organizing principle of modern society; he understood that a strong social contract was an essential foundation or core.

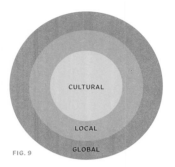

CULTURAL

LOCAL

GLOBAL

FIG. 9

Or, like this. (FIG. 9)

Thinking globally and acting locally has been a catchphrase for a few generations, now, but it is too easy to forget that at the heart of the matter is culture. It does little good to go local if local is just a mechanical translation of global market mentality at a smaller scale. CULTURE is what keeps LOCAL from becoming just a crude, propinquitous expression of the GLOBAL or, worse, from sliding into the parochial, the provincial, and the xenophobic.

* * * * *

Will nurture capital mature into a full-fledged sector that takes its rightful place alongside venture capital and philanthropy? A small cadre of nurture capital intermediaries is emerging, creating new ways to support healthy agriculture, without the imperatives of global capital markets unduly influencing investees to accelerate growth, reduce biodiversity, or avert their gaze from local markets. Iroquois Valley Farms, Dirt Capital, RSF Social Finance, and Farmland LP each address particular pieces of the funding puzzle for local food systems and organic farms. Cutting Edge Capital designs and implements community capital offerings, working with mission-driven enterprises to raise money from wealthy and retail individuals in their locales; many of their clients have been food businesses. Organic Valley isn't local, and isn't a financial intermediary, but it is bringing to market the dairy and meat products of 2,000 small organic farms and doing so through cooperative ownership, creating a way for more than 4,000 investors to provide $111 million to support their growth along the way. Similarly, Equal Exchange doesn't address the local piece, but it is pioneering food entrepreneurship and social finance; the 25-year-old worker-cooperative imports and sells Fair Trade coffee, chocolate, and tea, has grown to $70 million in sales, and offers small investors the opportunity to participate via pooled Certificates of Deposit.

Beyond food and agriculture, a growing number of investors, philanthropists, companies, and NGOs are working, directly or indirectly, in nurture capitalistic ways along the boundaries of investing and philanthropy—mission-related investing by foundations, impact investing, ecological economics, Investors' Circle, Newman's Own, Give Something Back, BALLE, Transition Towns, Social Venture Partners, B Lab, giving circles, Kickstarter, and Kiva. Nurture capital approaches can be applied to many areas of local economic, cultural, and ecological health, such as distributed renewable energy projects, local newspapers, independent media, affordable housing, and community health services.

* * * * *

The challenges of doing all this while working in an institutional context are obvious. Even a charitable foundation, and one focused on sustainable agriculture at that, faces many challenges along the path to nurture capital.

In 1994, the Jessie Smith Noyes Foundation set out on this path, and while some of the issues we dealt with (I was, at that time, the foundation's treasurer) are particular to the structure and function of foundations, the broader process of what the foundation called "dissonance reduction" is the soil in which nurture capital is rooted. The following essay from the foundation's 1994 Annual Report is a valuable statement of first principles.

> The goal of the Jessie Smith Noyes Foundation is to prevent irreversible damage to natural systems and ensure a sustainable society. Until recently, our only tool was grantmaking. Now, we have begun to explore how the management of our assets can also be used as an instrument for achieving our mission. In so doing, we have begun to re-examine aspects of corporate culture and fiduciary responsibility which we had held to be axiomatic. This essay, written jointly by the President and Treasurer of the foundation, reflects our commitment to this process.
>
> ---
>
> **Dissonance, Responsibility and Corporate Culture,**
> **Or, How Two Camps Struggle for Our Hearts and Minds**
> **and What We Can Do About It**
>
> Ours is an age of dissonance.
>
> We know that atmospheric pollution poses a significant and potentially irreversible threat, yet gasoline tax hikes are politically unacceptable and surveys show that increases of a dime a gallon for ultra-low emission gas formulations are resisted by consumers.
>
> We know that petrochemicals threaten our groundwater, yet we apply fertilizers and herbicides to our lawns and import bottled drinking water from afar.

We know that cigarette smoking causes cancer, yet we value the stock of the corporations that make them in the many billions of dollars and include the growth and profitability of these companies in measures of national economic health.

Reflecting this pervasive dissonance, foundations often find themselves in the position of supporting with their investment dollars activities that are antithetical to the charitable purpose of their grantmaking. By accepting as axiomatic the Iron Curtain between making money and giving it away, foundations reinforce the kind of corporate culture that identifies corporate responsibility with financial management, relegating social and environmental problems to the provinces of politics and philanthropy.

At the Jessie Smith Noyes Foundation, we have found our way to such questions on both the theoretical and practical levels. In theory, we have become convinced that traditional economic models are fundamentally flawed by their failure to take into account the long-term impact of economic growth on communities and the environment. In practice, we found ourselves owning shares of a company whose environmental impact and lack of responsiveness to community concerns were being contested by a coalition of our grantees.

Once recognized, this dissonance becomes undeniable on both levels. By investing with the sole aim of economic self-interest, we would endorse the market orthodoxies in which all growth is good and any contradictions are explained away as "side effects" and "externalities." By profiting from passively holding stock of a company whose environmental impact is being challenged by one of our grantees, we would put our self-interest before the interests of our grantees. Once recognized, the dissonance becomes defining: the only desirable actions are those which reduce it.

But moving towards "dissonance reduction" is an uncertain process for a foundation Board. The cultural barriers between finance committees and grantmakers are usually impenetrable. Many on the program side have little interest or experience in investing and do not know the language of finance. For those on the investment side, fragmentary or insufficient performance data for "social investment" seem to confirm their assumption that the introduction of so-called exogenous factors into investment decision-making reduces the universe and limits returns.

Underlying differences of vocabulary and training runs a fault line, a difference of thinking and perception that tends to push us as decision makers into two distinct camps:

Camp One. If you believe either that indefinite expansion of consumption on a finite planet is a physical impossibility, or that quality is fundamentally independent of (or, after a point of diminishing returns, in inverse relation to) quantity, then economic growth and profit-maximizing are no longer synonymous with progress or fiduciary responsibility.

Camp Two. If you believe that scientific advance, technological breakthrough and entrepreneurial creativity are engines of continued improvement of the human condition, or that lack of faith in the capacity of innovation to overcome obstacles is a greater problem than the obstacles themselves, then economic growth and profit-maximizing remain the *sine qua non* of progress and fiduciary responsibility.

While on one level it takes considerable commitment and dedication for Board members to resist falling into one or the other ideological camp, on another level the dissonance remains quite concrete:

— Should a health funder own stock in a tobacco company?

— Should a foundation pursuing disarmament own stock in a munitions manufacturer?

— Can an environmental grantmaker own shares of a major oil company?

— How about the oil company that rates best in terms of compliance with environmental regulations or is the first in the industry to sign the CERES Principles?

The shades of gray multiply rapidly, and it is for this reason that many in the financial community are quick to dismiss "social investment'" as subjective, difficult to quantify and unwieldy as a portfolio management tool. Yet it has been our experience that while we seldom arrive at clear cut decisions in particular cases, the process itself is a meaningful one and leads us to central and far-reaching questions: Can companies balance the social and environmental needs of the community in which they are located with the imperatives of distant shareholders and financial markets? Is "environmentalism" something that can be "afforded" by small companies and job-starved communities? Such questions lie at the heart of our purpose. For if we are "to prevent irreversible damage to the natural systems upon which all life depends," and if we believe that in the coming century economic activity will create ecological and political stresses of global proportions, then it is no longer prudent to keep philanthropy and investment separate. We must seek to affect the way all corporations and financial institutions understand their responsibility. We must help all businesses acknowledge and then deal with the dissonance between shareholder value and the social and environmental costs of commercial activity, costs that are not reflected on corporate balance sheets. And we must, of course, begin by putting our own house in order.

We wish to acknowledge just how small the steps we have taken are, especially when measured against the scale of the problems they seek to address. This a learning process. We are a financial institution with less than $60 million under management. Many questions remain, particularly around issues of how to measure the impact of our investments on environment and community.

But we are committed to the task of dissonance reduction at the Noyes Foundation: to use asset management *and* grantmaking as instruments of change. We welcome collaboration with other financial institutions and for-profit and non-profit organizations who wish to work with us in addressing the fundamental questions:

— What *kind* of companies do we wish to support?

— What *kind* of corporate culture do we wish to encourage?

— What *kind* of economy do we wish to build, and, through it, what *kind* of communities and world shall we attempt to shape?[13]

13   1994 Annual Report of the Jessie Smith Noyes Foundation, Stephen Viederman (President) and Woody Tasch (Treasurer)

Such thinking bumps up against the limits of institutional innovation. How far can foundations go in reimagining their structure and function? Perhaps some philanthropy can be aimed at seeding wholly new kinds of institutions. **Decelerators**— academies for farmers, food entrepreneurs, investors, and donors who want to build local food systems and find other ways to slow some of their money down. **Slow Munis**—municipal bonds that finance food hubs, farmers markets, and CSAs. **A. Corporations** (A. for altruistic)—companies that follow the lead of Newman's Own, giving away 100% of their profits, or perhaps companies that pick up on the Slow Money Principles, giving away 50% of their profits (for every dollar of fast money going to shareholders, a dollar of slow money going to soil and community).

Institutions, like planets, have limits. The work of foundations integrating investing and grantmaking is important not only because it tests the limits of corporate culture, but also because it points to the work we must each do as individuals, integrating heart and mind, moving back and forth between left brain and right, and summoning the imagination to put institutional thinking in its place, so that we may reconnect with one another in the places where we live.

* * * * *

A foundation plowing new ground between grantmaking and investing is one thing, an organic farmer sitting between horse and plow, another. Recently, I spoke with one such farmer.

Her name is Zoë Bradbury. She grew up on the southern Oregon coast, birthing lambs in the spring, watching salmon spawn in the fall, and canning plums and tomatoes all summer. After Stanford University and a stint in the nonprofit world, she returned. Since 2008, she has run a diversified, fresh-market farm on land shared with her mother and sister. Zoë cultivates a couple hundred varieties of vegetable, berry, fruit, herb, and flower crops for her CSA, supplies local restaurants, grocery stores, and foodbanks, and runs a farm stand and u-pick. She cultivates with horse power whenever possible.

WT   **In my day, we had a word, *countercultural*. You don't hear it any more. Do you think that applies to what you are doing? Is a small organic farm— using horse power when you can—countercultural?**

ZB   I suppose so, if you define culture as mainstream American farming.

WT   **What do you mean by mainstream American farming?**

ZB   Big equipment, monocrops, glyphosate, commodity markets. If that's culture—if that's where most American calories come from—then we are *countercultural*.

Zoë Bradbury

WT **Funny, the way you said it, "if that's where most of the calories come from..." That's quite a quantitative definition of culture, isn't it?**

ZB I guess it is. All the mainstream calories are subsidized. What would the food on our plates look like if the government subsidized what we small, organic farmers are growing instead? If energy, corn, and soy weren't subsidized? I'm not saying I wish we were subsidized—and the good news is I don't need a government subsidy in order to make a living. I'm grateful for that.

WT **One person's making a living is another person's—*what*? Countercultural adventure?**

ZB Coming home to start up a small-farm business has been quite an adventure. Most days you depend on natural forces beyond your control to make your living. The money part has definitely been a wild ride, particularly in the beginning. The financial stress of farming doesn't ever go away completely. We have good years and we have bad years. We have business growth spurts that require elusive capital, and we routinely weather unforeseen, expensive disasters: hurricanes, floods, droughts, barn fires, broken tie-rods, runaway horses, diesel thieves, global economic meltdowns, cucumber beetle infestations, hungry deer, and the neighbor's bloodthirsty dog. Sometimes things knock us flat, but they don't leave us completely broke or broken.

WT **What does making a living mean to you in terms of money?**

ZB I value lifestyle more than money, but I care that the farm is profitable for the sake of paying a living wage to our crew, for the sake of succeeding as a small business, for the sake of being able to afford a few weeks of vacation each winter. It's a fun challenge, particularly in an out-of-the-way rural place like ours. This isn't Portland or San Francisco in terms of having millions of potential mouths to feed who want to eat from local farms.

We're on the southern Oregon coast up Floras Creek a few miles from Langlois, a town of a few hundred. The nearest markets are a string of small coastal towns north and south of us from Gold Beach to Coos Bay. There are lots of cranberries grown for the commodity market in our area. There's livestock, cattle, sheep, hay, pastured chickens, and eggs in the region—not much veggie production. We sell to a handful of grocery stores and food co-ops. We also have some wonderful long-term relationships with restaurants.

My sister, mom, and I run four businesses. We each have a farm business and then everyone markets under the fourth business, which is Valley Flora—our distribution entity and brand. My farm entity supports me, one full-time employee, and a few part-time employees. My husband has an off-farm job. We have 115 members in our CSA. On a summer day, we have about 70 customers show up at the farm stand.

We grow five acres of diversified vegetables and have a few acres of orchard. We are in the process of developing another nine acres across the road in order to improve our crop rotation, grow more of our own fertility, and keep a third of the farm in the year-round cover crop.

Our sales are half CSA, with the other half split 60/40 between sales to restaurants and our farm stand. It all adds up to around $200,000 a year in sales, with my farm making up 68% of that. The rest is from my mom's and sister's operations.

WT   When you graduated from Stanford, did you know you were going to end up back on your family farm?

ZB   Not at all. I launched out of school to save the world via non-profit work. I did a stint in Minneapolis at the Institute for Agriculture and Trade Policy. Then I went to the Bay Area and worked for ALBA (the Agriculture and Land-based Training Association) and the Center for Urban Education about Sustainable Agriculture, which was then spearheading the development of the Ferry Building. Years later, I went back to see the place.

WT   And what did you think?

ZB   My first question was, "Wow! How was this financed?" My opinion of the Ferry Building would be heavily influenced by knowing how it was financed. Public dollars? Private investment? I'm not sure public dollars should go to such a high-end commercial venue. Even at my level—and I consider myself middle class—I have to keep my hand on my wallet when I'm there. I chew my cud a lot about the whole elite charge and the organic food movement. The Ferry Building is beautiful and there's certainly a public awareness component, but I'm not quite sure what to make of it in terms of the balance of elitism and greater access to good food.

Public funds shouldn't exacerbate wealth disparity. There's already too much of it. But the Ferry Building is a very beautiful public space. Lots to marvel at. One

Violetto artichokes

shop had a basket of five violetto artichokes for $9 a pound on a chic display shelf. That didn't quite seem like a real food-buying experience. Actually, I get more excited by putting together a CSA box.

WT **When I'm in the Ferry Building—and I have to say that two of my favorite restaurants in the world are there, Hog Island Oysters and Boulettes Larder—I cannot help but think that we, the many tens of millions of Americans who own stock, and also the much narrower we, the one percent who own a wildly disproportionate amount of that stock, we like to wander through the food bazaar, consuming or just ogling the most expensive olive oil and wine and artisan cheese, while at the same time our investments are streaming to sweat shops in Bangladesh and smokestacks in China.**

ZB For me, that tension became apparent when I found myself working 60 hours a week at a nonprofit to change the world, but the 401K options that were offered to me were all traditional, all about getting the most bang for my retirement buck. Isn't this tragically hypocritical? Investing in the very things we are fighting to change.

What perfect job security! Feed the root of the problems that you spend all of your working days trying to fix.

I was dumbstruck. I couldn't invest. I decided I was unwilling to buy into the conventional stock market, even if it means having no retirement and being a destitute old geezer someday. I just can't compromise my values for the sake of personal gain. It's an ethical thing for me.

WT **How do you feel about elitism when you are at home on your farm?**

ZB The same issues permeate my thinking. A handful of our CSA members pay with food stamps and we take WIC (Women, Infants, and Children nutritional program subsidies) at our farm stand. Of our members, 70% pay in full at the beginning of the season—$800 for 28 weeks. The other 30% pay on a monthly pay plan. When I go to the grocery store, I'm struck by how expensive comparable food to ours is in the store. We sell a head of lettuce for $2.50 at our farm stand, but it's the size of a beach ball. In the store, for $2.99, there's a much smaller head of lettuce that is tired, wilted, conventionally-grown produce and you have no idea where it came from. So that makes me less self-conscious about our prices. It makes me feel like we are providing a great value. I also have to remind myself that it is not only the farmer's job to make food affordable—we need to do our best to be careful stewards who produce high-quality calories as efficiently as possible.

But access to food is also a conversation about living wage, overlooked expensive externalities, and government policy that for decades has favored and subsidized big and corporate. I would love to know how much a bag of Fritos or a McDonald's burger and fries would really cost if you took away corn and soy subsidies, if you paid everyone who helped produce, process, and serve it a living wage, and if you were paying for the environmental and health externalities of conventional agriculture, dead zones in the Gulf of Mexico, obesity and diabetes epidemics, antibiotic resistance, loss of biodiversity, etc., etc.

I read a study that said the true cost of a Big Mac is $12 if you factor in all the environmental, health, and subsidy externalities, not $4.50. That means we're all out seven bucks every time McDonald's sells a burger. Not to pick on Mickey D's too much, but I can get a local, grass-fed burger with organic greens on organic bread for $10 here in Langlois at our greasy spoon. Whoever labeled the organic/sustainable food movement as elitist was conveniently not looking at the whole price tag of conventional food. Unfortunately, despite these facts, the label has stuck.

And there was nothing elitist about the way we funded ourselves at the start.

I saved, I penny-pinched, I scrapped and scavenged in anticipation of the cash outlay it would take to get the farm off the ground. Nevertheless, come April, I had spent everything and my first hope of income was still two months out, growing slowly through a cold, wet spring. I had hoped to qualify for a USDA Beginning Farmer Loan, a federal program that until then had stirred up feelings of pride and patriotism in me. What a great government to earmark funding specifically to support young farmers! But when I told the loan officer that I needed the money to pay for a buried irrigation mainline on the family land I was row-cropping, he shook his head unapologetically. "Sorry, no money for permanent improvements on leased land." No matter that it was family land that I intended to lease for a lifetime, and maybe someday own. Never mind that I was the very demographic they were purporting to serve—a young, limited-resource female who was just starting out. It was a bitter pill, getting a USDA slapdown in my very first season.

I resorted to a 12-month, 0% credit card to finance my first year of farming—the scariest, most out-on-a-limb financial risk I'd ever taken. Thanks be to a good growing season, I was able to pull myself out of credit card debt before the 18.9% interest rate kicked in. Then, we started our CSA and that became my bank.

No, despite my concerns about elitism, my passion for farming and for the movement is alive and well.

WT **The movement?**

ZB Regenerative agriculture—leaving things better than we found them. All those years in college were in the context of something called sustainability. But sustainability's not adequate, given the challenges of climate change. So, I keep taking the farm more aggressively towards less till, year-round cover crops, thinking about what we can do to nurture the soil for the really long haul. That's what the new nine acres we're expanding to are all about. Growing more of our own fertility. Feels like we are still on the very tip of farming as well as we might be doing. There's still so much more to do if we are going to make a real difference.

Zoë and the Valley Flora team

* * * * *

If we are going to get meaningful flows of nurture capital going to the Bradburys and Butterworks of the world, we're going to need ground rules that, from a Wall Street perspective, may indeed look countercultural. Such ground rules would describe a kind of "CSA of investing," organized around the following attributes:

Grassroots. From the bottom, up. Not just for folks who already think of themselves as investors.

About putting back in at least as much as taking out. Some (or more than some) financial returns stay in.

Local. Businesses that stay put, oriented around community and place.

Small. Is beautiful.

Slow. Long-term, intergenerational, respecting natural rhythms and cycles. Financial compost.

Convivial. Face-to-face. Breaking bread whenever possible.

Diverse. Beyond diversified and decentralized. Economically, ecologically, and culturally diverse.

Democratic. Participatory decision-making. Civic engagement as important as capital flow.

Peaceable and neighborly. Wendell Berry bumper stickers available.

Anti-financial-razzmatazz and pro-earthworm. Gary Nabhan bumper stickers allowed.[14]

Inclined to regularly and vigorously reaffirm the difference between bullshit and horseshit. Zoë Bradbury bumper stickers required.

Not exactly Robert's Rules of Order or The Prudent Man Rule.

* * * * *

The above list of attributes should also include **Feminine.**

Leslie Christian, former CEO of Portfolio 21 and an advisor at NorthStar Asset Management, and Kelley Buhles, Senior Director of Philanthropic Services & Organizational Culture at RSF Social Finance, propose moving from the Prudent Man Rule to the Prudent Woman Rule:

> The world of investing abides by various rules. Some are defined and articulated in formal legislation and regulations, while others are based on customs, common practices, and opinions expressed by jurists in court cases. The expectation of "prudence" in financial management is one such case.[15]
>
> Originally expressed as the "Prudent Man Rule," this standard—put simply—requires fiduciaries to consider various economic, risk, and liquidity factors as they relate to their clients or beneficiaries, and to invest accordingly. The Uniform Prudent Investor Act, adopted in the 1990s, allows investors to use the principles of Modern Portfolio Theory (MPT), including a total return approach to investing and an emphasis on diversification, as a means of achieving "prudent" fiduciary decisions. The act invited women into the

14   Gary Nabhan is often referred to as the father of the local food movement. He is W.K. Kellogg Endowed Chair in Sustainable Food Systems at the University of Arizona, author of several award-winning books, and an emeritus board member of the Slow Money Institute.

15   "All that can be required of a trustee is that he shall conduct himself faithfully and exercise a sound discretion. He is to observe how men of prudence, discretion, and intelligence manage their own affairs, not in regard to speculation, but in regard to the permanent disposition of their funds, considering the probable income as well as the probable safety of the capital to be invested... Do what you will, the capital is at hazard." https://en.wikipedia.org/wiki/Harvard_College_v._Amory

equation, only linguistically, by referencing a "prudent person" rather than a "prudent man." Although "man" was ditched for the gender-neutral term, the thinking and theory were not broadened to include the feminine.

For decades, there was an explicit expectation that men set the standard for prudence: "to observe how men of prudence, discretion, and intelligence manage their own affairs." While the concept of the "prudent woman" may be interpreted as the opposite extreme, we choose this term for our theory over a gender-less alternative because we've seen how semantics can hide the truth. We've observed that the dominant economic paradigm still reflects what are traditionally considered masculine traits. We wonder what value feminine traits might bring to our increasingly challenging economic situation. In other words, is it time to ask, "What would a prudent woman do?"

One of the ironies of the Prudent Man Rule in economics is that the word "economy" derives from the Greek word that means "management of the household." In our contemporary world, management of the household has become "home economics," a term associated with "women's work," usually unpaid and undervalued. Meanwhile, men dominate the system that we now call economics, that is, the making and exchanging of goods and services in the pursuit of maximum profit.

The market economy, the milieu of the prudent man, has become the lens through which we view our entire world. It is the first and foremost arbiter of ideas and proposals ranging from personal career choices to public policy. Unless an idea makes economic sense, it is subject to ridicule and trivialization. Those who dare to question the superiority of the economy are considered naïve. This is especially true when it comes to investing. The power of assumptions about the purpose of investing is so great that there is virtually no room for disagreement or debate among the professional cadre of advisors, managers, and other practitioners. These embedded assumptions are then transmitted to and imposed upon the clients who place their trust in these professionals. This circle is reinforced by self-interest and fueled by the allure of wealth and power.

We think this has gone too far. Witness the corruption of our democracy by money and greed, the depletion of our natural resources, the poisoning of people and planet, and the vulgar inequality driven by capitalism run amok and rudderless. These are the real risks to the future of investing and the economy.

The world of business and finance has generally been unappreciative of feminine traits, and many women and men have suppressed these aspects of themselves in an effort to conform to the dominant culture. Furthermore, women are often stereotyped in ways that are simplistic, judgmental, and demeaning. What if we could snap our fingers and instantly transform these stereotypes of women into positive character traits of value and power? What if women's ways were the ways of business and investing? We wonder what would happen if the prudent woman stepped in.

Let us be clear: we are not talking about how women can conform to the current world of investing, nor are we promoting gender lens investing. We are talking about the unmitigated feminine—unharnessed, unjudged, and unconstrained. In a system that is so heavily skewed toward the masculine, we think a shift toward the feminine—by women and men alike—would be healthy and prudent.

We offer below our take on what it might mean to work with an investment framework that is founded on feminine traits. We have used research into cultural stereotypes and generalizations regarding what is "feminine" and what is "masculine" as a foundation. We recognize and appreciate that these are stereotypes. Feminine traits are, of course, not limited to women just as masculine traits are not limited to men.

To start, let's look at some of the key character traits that are typically ascribed to men and women. The following information was compiled from studying 64,000 people and published in The Athena Doctrine.[16]

16   *The Athena Doctrine*, John Gerzema and Michael D'Antonio (Young & Rubicam Brands and Jossey-Bass, 2013)

"Masculine" Traits
— Decisive
— Logical
— Strong
— Proud and confident
— Independent, self-reliant
— Stubborn
— Rigid
— Unapproachable

- Focused, driven, and straightforward
- Selfish and competitive
- Aggressive
- Assertive

"Feminine" Traits
- Curious
- Intuitive
- Vulnerable
- Humble
- Community oriented, team player
- Imaginative
- Sensitive
- Open to new ideas
- Plans for the future
- Helpful and nurturing
- Patient
- Listens

From these traits, we can envision an alternative, feminine way of thinking about economics:

- Economics is a human construct that is as fluid as human behavior, not a science that operates by certain fixed and "natural" laws.
- We can live in an economic matriarchy based on trust, collaboration, and connection, not an economic patriarchy that thrives on competition, fear, and marginalization of the other.
- Small is beautiful, and growth is not necessarily good or proof of success and worth.
- Modern Portfolio Theory is only as real as its underlying assumptions, which are merely assumptions, not facts, that have been constructed to make the theory work. We should directly challenge the belief that MPT is real and grounded in mathematics and certainty.

The ideas we describe above are not radical or unrealistic. They are simply more "feminine" than "masculine" and have not been part of the mainstream financial culture of our modern world. Once we open ourselves to these alternative ways of approaching economics, we also become open to a different way of thinking about investing and the standards that could apply to a prudent investor. The Prudent Woman Rule for investing might look like this:

— A prudent woman takes investing personally while also considering the whole. This means living with contradiction and uncertainty; refusing to ignore or justify that which is difficult, unfamiliar, or frightening; and analyzing the implications of every investment in terms of who benefits and who gets hurt in the generation of financial returns.
— A prudent woman cares about justice and fairness and considers these to be critical factors in decisions related to money and investing. She knows when enough is enough, and willingly enters into a process of divesting and giving as a way of addressing inequity.
— A prudent woman educates herself on the origins of wealth; the history of colonization, slavery, and capitalism; gift economies; and other relevant aspects of our modern economy and its alternatives, in order to understand the context and implications of investing.
— A prudent woman does what she can and is content with small solutions rather than grandiose ambitions and gestures.
— A prudent woman speaks out and stands up for her approach.

During these trying times, we invite those who have access to wealth of any size to bring a Prudent Woman framework to your investing. We encourage you to have challenging conversations with your investment advisors and financial managers, to question preconceptions about the "rules" of investing, and to imagine what else is not just possible but also valuable and beneficial. Through thoughtful and daring investments, we can build a new field of finance and a new economy based on love, respect, and interdependence.[17]

17   https://outsideinvestments.com/ prudent-woman/

Prudence also dictates preserving and restoring soil fertility, a fact which, happily, is not lost on earthworms who, as humble, hard-working hermaphrodites, pretty much have both sides of the nurture capital question nailed.

* * * * *

As Oscar Wilde put it, "The whole problem with socialism is that it requires too many evening meetings." While nurture capital is not socialism, it is a highly sociable form of capitalism and the point is well taken. At the Noyes Foundation, we did not document the hours, days, and months required by the process of dissonance reduction. We invested them enthusiastically. Where did this enthusiasm come from? It came from affection. It came from the knowledge that, however crude our manifestations, we were moving in the direction of affection.

For the budding nurture capitalist, looking ahead to meetings, to the investment of time and energy as well as money, the question is obvious: Is it really worth the effort? What we are contemplating cannot compare to the efficiency and the partially sublimated adrenaline rush of speculation afforded by buying shares of Alibaba on E*Trade. Is nurture capital really worth the time and trouble?

Not if you are measuring by the metrics of transactions. But if you are non-measuring by the non-metrics of relationships, oh, yes, it is more than worth it.

If you are non-measuring by the non-standards of innate value, yes, it is more than worth it.

If you are non-measuring in pursuit of nonviolence, yes, again.

If you are non-measuring in the name of the beauty of organic beets and heirloom seeds and water in aquifers and food in food deserts and organic matter in the soil, then, yes, it is more than worth it.

* * * * *

Wendell Berry lovers of the world, what are we going to invest in? CSA members and farmers market shoppers, what in the world are we going to invest in? Slow Food folk, members of Wedge and La Montanita and Mountain People's cooperatives, patrons of farm to table restaurants, supporters of Farm Aid and American Farmland Trust and Marin Agricultural Land Trust and Sustainable Iowa Land Trust and Seed Savers Exchange, lobbyists for a new Farm Bill, 350.orgers, Occupiers and angry voters, localists and globalists, Prudent Men and Women, what in the world are we going to invest in?

We begin here—putting our affection and some of our money to work near where we live, in things that we understand, in food and soil.

IV Hereabouts

As surely as a home is far more than a house, the place where I live is far more than a street, a town, a county, a country, a zip code, or an IP address. I don't live in the land of politics or the realm of economics. I don't live inside the Beltway or in Nasdaqland or Kazakhstan. I don't live in cyberspace.

I live on two acres, here, in the Front Range of the Rocky Mountains, at around 8,000 feet, abutting a hundred acres of pasture and a decent size spring, under the outcroppings that go by the white man's name of Twin Sisters. One of these days, I'd like to poke around and see if I might discover an Arapaho name for this place, this pacific, grassy glade, this gentle meadow bowl beneath the rocks, beautiful today as it has been for millions of years, west of the Flatirons and east of the Continental Divide, five or ten miles, as the magpie flies, from where Boulder Creek spills out of the foothills and onto the plains.

Although I've lived here for six years, I barely know this place. As to its human inhabitants, forget it: Mountain folk prize privacy. Only twice has my doorstep been graced with unexpected visitors. Once, seeking directions. The second time, seeking to give direction—biblical direction, that is.

With respect to flora and fauna, water and soil, I've only scratched the surface. I've put in eight raised beds with hoops, brought in compost and organic soil amendments, and keep a compost tumbler busy. Garlic does fine up here. So does kale. And, yes, it's true that I did, last summer, enjoy a harvest of seven cherry tomatoes. I worshipped them briefly and then ate them. In summer, I am grateful for indian paint brush, blanket flower, columbine, mountain aster, California poppy, yarrow, and others whose names I don't yet know. In winter, I decipher tracks in the snow of coyote, bobcat, chipmunk, squirrel, rabbit, and deer. I enjoy the episodic acquaintance of scores of elk during shoulder seasons.

At a time when the real is being threatened by the fake, nothing is more important than zooming back in to where we live.

* * * * *

Quite the flap about fake news, real news, and tweeting has been flapping for many months now:

> Fake news, and the proliferation of raw opinion that passes for news, is creating confusion, punching holes in what is true, causing a kind of fun-house effect that leaves the reader doubting everything, including real news.

> That has pushed up the political temperature and increased polarization. No longer burdened with wrestling with the possibility that they might be wrong, people on the right and the left have become more entrenched in their positions, experts say. In interviews, people said they felt more empowered, more attached to their own side and less inclined to listen to the other. Polarization is fun, like cheering a goal for the home team.[1]

And:

> A great paradox of our hyper-connected digital age is that we seem to be drifting apart. Increasingly, however, research confirms our deepest intuition: Human connection lies at the heart of human well-being. It's up to all of us—doctors, patients, neighborhoods and communities—to maintain bonds where they're fading, and create ones where they haven't existed.[2]

While I was reading stories such as these, a piece about Twinkies and private equity investing also caught my attention:

> For all the profits Apollo and Metropoulos squeezed out of the Hostess factories, a deal hatched in a hotel room on Fifth Avenue in New York shows how private equity can have its snack cake and eat it, too. There, in the Versailles Room at the St. Regis, Apollo and Metropoulos began the process of extracting returns from the company, less than a year after shutting the Schiller Park plant.

> Most investors seeking profit have to wait for the right moment to sell a company or take it public. But private equity uses a different playbook. First, Apollo and Metropoulos arranged for Hostess to borrow money from the banking giant Credit Suisse. The two firms then pocketed about $900 million of that money for themselves and their investors. Hostess, meanwhile, is stuck repaying the debt.

> This type of deal is known as a dividend recapitalization, and it is a staple of private equity's money-making strategy. These deals provide private equity firms an opportunity to profit before they even sell a company, an added bonus to

1   "As Fake News Spreads Lies, More Readers Shrug at the Truth," Sabrina Tavernise, Dec. 6, 2016, *New York Times*

2   "How Social Isolation Is Killing Us," Dhruv Khullar, December 22, 2016, *New York Times*

the firms and their investors, including public pensioners. Since 2012, private equity firms have arranged hundreds of such deals, totaling over $148 billion in debt, according to Thomson Reuters. Hostess's dividend deal was the third largest of 2015.[3]

3   "How the Twinkie Made the Superrich Even Richer," Michael Corkery and Ben Protess, December 10, 2016, *New York Times*

Private equity investors recapitalize Hostess; food technologists reconfigure Twinkies. Recently the shelf life of the famous snack has been extended from 26 to 65 days (although urban legend continues to cite far longer periods).

Fake news. Fake food. Fake investing. Connect the dots.

Which might not seem to have much to do with the places where we live, but it does. These are the forces—media, capital markets, commodification, industrialization—that divert our attention from *here*. We are busy feeding ourselves a steady diet of the fake, the manufactured, and the fast.

* * * * *

Do we need a new economic theory to rediscover sense of place? A new political ideology to restore community and build soil fertility? Based on my interactions with many thousands of folks and the emergence of slow money investing around the country and beyond, my answer would be no. We do not need a new theory or a new ideology in order to take the first steps in a new direction.

There are millions of folks who already think Wendell Berry is right, who think Eisenhower was right when he warned us about the military-industrial complex, who think Thoreau and Gandhi and Schumacher and Bill McKibben were and are right, who still think of Joni Mitchell's "For Free" now and again, who have had their thinking profoundly influenced by Donella Meadows,[4] who are grateful to M.C. Escher for demonstrating that up and down, left and right, foreground and background should not be taken for granted, who consider Christopher Alexander's *A Pattern Language* iconic, who love Hazel Henderson, who laughed so hard at Firesign Theatre and Monty Python and George Carlin that they thought the triumph of the counterculture was inevitable, who quote Martin Luther King Jr. whenever given half a chance, who can't get Joel Salatin's enactment of soil critters out of their head, who think a crusty loaf of organic sourdough bread is a thing of beauty, who have a penchant for independent bookstores, who think Joan Gussow is a guru and Eliot Coleman an authentic pioneer, who would admire Zoë Bradbury greatly if they met her, who experience viscerally a kind of Great Anthropocene Cognitive Dissonance in the face of climate change, the invasion of the real by the virtual, the idea of drones delivering organic pizza, and other such predicaments of

4   Donella H. "Dana" Meadows was a pioneering American environmental scientist, teacher, and writer. She is best known as lead author of *The Limits to Growth* and author of *Thinking in Systems: a Primer*.

the contemporary kind, and who sense that building local food systems and putting their hands in the soil are acts both simple and far-reaching.

And yet... and yet... our money remains in the hands of fiduciaries and financial institutions.

This is a job that is going to require pragmatism and poetry.

* * * * *

Poetry may be the only thing strong enough to blast barnacles off the hull of 20th century economic thinking. Poetry is an antidote to It's the Economy, Stupid. It's biodiesel for tired old mental tractors. It's mobile chicken coops for the McNugget-minded. Poetry is the opposite of warring sound bites, disclaimers, legalese, appendices, indices, punditries, fiduciaryese, demagogueries, pre-transaction niceties, CEO and investment banker salaries, insect-size computerized flying pollinating machineries that are touted as the bee's knees, and manufactured cheese product pretending to be cheese.

So, I find myself, here—here in my heart, here where I live, here (to use a military metaphor that is surely as incongruous as a dollar bill in a compost pile) on the beach where I've landed, here after decades of work at the nexus of socially responsible investing, venture capital, and philanthropy—tending, with a sense of renewal, gratitude, and a slight palpitation of the heart, towards the poetically incorrect.

Because I want to get beyond the politically correct and the economically correct.

Because I don't want Twinkies, terrorism, and tweets to have sovereignty over my thoughts.

Because I need more than, "Campaign in Poetry, Govern in Prose."

Because the road to cultural healing is paved not only with compelling ideological arguments and earnest manifestos, but also with playful musings, quirky quasi-divinities, and organic beets.

* * * * *

My bookshelves are filled with solemn diagnoses and sober treatises. Many argue eloquently that the worldview and narratives that got us here are no longer appropriate for the circumstances of the 21st century. They call for a new Anthropocene narrative.[5] They trace our uneven progress from Manifest Destiny, Two Cars in Every Garage and a Chicken in Every Pot, the American Dream, and the Invisible Hand towards a new era of what the Club of Rome calls *Limits to Growth*, what Janine Benyus calls *Biomimicry*, what Van Jones calls *The Green Collar Economy*, what Allan Savory calls *Holistic Management*, what Bill Mollison and David Holmgren call *Permaculture One*, what Gary Nabhan calls *Cultures of Habitat*, what Herman Daly calls *Steady-State Economics,* and others call degrowth or "The Great Deceleration," what Bill McKibben calls *Deep Economy*, what E.O. Wilson calls *Consilience*, and what Dee Hock, the founder of Visa, calls *Birth of the Chaordic Age*.

Sweeping references to economic and environmental history seem awfully far-reaching for a discussion of something as seemingly inconsequential as making some 0% loans to local farmers. That may be so, particularly if one's view of the consequential is framed by billions of dollars and trillions of dollars. Yet it is entirely possible, at this moment in history, that what we are up to, we nurture capitalists, we who would slow some of our money down, we who want to know where our food comes from and where our money goes, is consequential precisely because it is *not* framed by billions of dollars and trillions of dollars. Remember, E.F. Schumacher, whose *Small Is Beautiful* is a book of particular consequence, remarked that if everything were small, he would have been arguing in favor of big.

Which is why what follows is not an investment prospectus, but, rather, a local invitation.

* * * * *

5 "According to the International Union of Geological Sciences (IUGS), the professional organization in charge of defining Earth's time scale, we are officially in the Holocene ('entirely recent') epoch, which began 11,700 years ago after the last major ice age. But that label is outdated, some experts say. They argue for 'Anthropocene'—from *anthropo*, for 'man,' and *cene*, for 'new'—because human-kind has caused mass extinctions of plant and animal species, polluted the oceans and altered the atmosphere, among other lasting impacts. Anthropocene has become an environmental buzzword ever since the atmospheric chemist and Nobel laureate Paul Crutzen popularized it in 2000. This year, the word has picked up velocity in elite science circles: It appeared in nearly 200 peer-reviewed articles, the publisher Elsevier has launched a new academic journal titled *Anthropocene* and the IUGS convened a group of scholars to decide [...] whether to officially declare that the Holocene is over and the Anthropocene has begun." (Joseph Stromberg, *Scientific American*, January 2013)

AN INVITATION

SOIL

SLOW OPPORTUNITIES FOR INVESTING LOCALLY

On The Joyful Task of Building Local Food Systems
(Including A Few Thoughts About Fake News, Real Food and Real Investing)

TO RESIDENTS OF BOULDER AND BEYOND

SLOWMONEY

Dear Neighbor,

We'd like to invite you to join us in pioneering a new way to support local food systems and sustainable agriculture on the Front Range. It's called Slow Opportunities for Investing Locally—SOIL.

This isn't *investing* in the traditional sense. We're using charitable donations and 0% loans to fund the next generation of diversified, organic farms and the small food enterprises that bring their produce to the local market. We're building a permanent, member-controlled funding resource. This is investing that leaves the returns in, for the benefit of future generations.

There are many social and environmental reasons why we are doing this. Climate Change. Nutrition. Community. There are also financial reasons. If we are going to do what needs to be done in the soil, then we are going to need to put aside some of our money in new ways.

This is what is driving Slow Money activities around the country. Since 2010, more than $57 million has flowed, via dozens of local networks, to 632 small food enterprises: Cheese makers, artisan bakers, heirloom seed companies, compost purveyors, small diversified organic farms (F.A.R.M.s,* too), grass-fed beef producers, goat dairies, yogurt companies, farm-to-table restaurants, probiotic pickleteers, community kitchens, regional grain mills, local distributors, inner city cooperatives and more.

Here in Colorado, hundreds of individuals have attended regional events or committed capital to Slow Money projects, including four investment clubs, resulting in the flow of $3.3 million to 36 local food deals. This money has flowed through peer-to-peer loans, angel investments and for-profit investment clubs. In 2015, we started our first non-profit investment club, 2Forks Club in Carbondale, and based on its success, we are now starting SOIL on the Front Range.

———————

Here's how it works.

> You become a member of SOIL with a tax deductible donation of $100 or more. Then, members make 0% loans to local farmers and food entrepreneurs, by majority vote—one member, one vote, no matter what the size of your donation. When loans are repaid, funds are recycled into new loans.

Zephyros Farm (left), a ten-year-old, four acre diversified organic farm in Paonia and the first certified organic flower producer in Colorado, received $23,500 to purchase a used refrigerated truck. Two Roots Farm (right), a start-up micro-farm in Carbondale, received $7,500 for drip irrigation and a walk-in cooler.

* F.A.R.M., in Boone, NC, is a café that allows customers to pay whatever they can afford: Food for All Regardless of Means. There is a network of such "one world cafes" around the country, some 70 or so strong. Denver's SAME Café (So All May Eat) is one. We haven't yet funded one of these cafés, but I hope we will soon.

Mountain Flower Goat Dairy (left) received a $43,000 0% loan to purchase processing equipment and plan for the establishment of a goat dairy cooperative. MM Local (right) received a $100,000 0% loan to assist in structuring their next round of financing.

We've been utilizing this model for the past two years over in the Roaring Fork Valley, where 33 individuals have contributed a total of $206,000, in amounts ranging from $100 to $80,000, to the 2Forks Club (named for the Roaring Fork River and the north fork of the Gunnison River). Seven loans have been made to date, with more in the pipeline.

"I've been farming for 20 years," says 2Forks member Brook Le Van, "And I've never seen anything this heartening in the way it connects people and supports the local food system. Especially in the current climate, with so much divisiveness and uncertainty, this is just what we all need."

Here on the Front Range, SOIL is starting off with $75,000 from a dozen founding members. I am joined on our launch committee by Brian Coppom (Executive Director, Boulder County Farmers' Market) and Amy Divine (Member, Women Donors Network). Helping us is a Kitchen Cabinet that includes a healthy handful of folks with experience in food and finance. We'd like to think that given population and geographical factors on the Front Range, we'll be able to achieve more scale than our sister group in the mountains, and that, over time, if enough of us keep at it, we can grow SOIL into a significant, community resource for funding local food systems, in Boulder and beyond.

The spirit behind SOIL is reflected in the Slow Money Principles, which start with "We must bring our money back down to earth" and end with:

> Paul Newman said, "In life, we need to be more like the farmer who puts back into the soil what he takes out." Recognizing the wisdom of these words, let us ask:
>
> • What would the world be like if we invested 50% of our assets within 50 miles of where we live?
> • What if there were a new generation of companies that gave away 50% of their profits?
> • What if there were 50% more organic matter in our soil 50 years from now?

Such questions point in a fundamentally new direction, although the actions we are taking—making small loans to farmers—are in many ways quite simple. This balance between big questions and small actions is central to the change we are seeking and the community we are building.

"Local food is all about relationships. As is soil fertility. We need a new kind of funding source that supports both. It's SOIL."
—Brian Coppom, Executive Director, Boulder County Farmers' Market

Slow Money investors have provided $275,000 to Poudre Valley Farms in Ft. Collins (left), pioneering a new model for community ownership of organic farmland. Re:Vision (right), which is developing a food coop in Denver's Westwood neighborhood, received a $50,000 grant by vote of attendees at a Slow Money event.

Here's another question, along with the partial answer that arises from slow money conversations:

Q. We're giving our money to people we don't know very well, to invest in things they don't understand very well, halfway around the world in places that most of us will never visit: Does this sound like the recipe for a healthy future?

A. Put our money to work in things that we understand, near where we live, starting with food.

It just may be that, led by farmers' markets and community supported agriculture and crowd funding and a few pioneering funds around the country, small food enterprises and local investing will mature over time as an asset class that produces predictable, risk-adjusted financial returns.

Or, it just may be that if we really want to nurture the slow, the small and the local, we'll just have to find the gumption to go slow, small and local with our money—using not only our consumer dollars, but our investment and philanthropy dollars, as well. We may just need to splice into our 20th century investment notions the principles of carrying capacity, care of the commons, sense of place, soil fertility, diversity and nonviolence.

Or . . . if that all sounds a bit much . . . we can just chip in to SOIL, enjoy getting together once in awhile, celebrate a little conviviality with our neighbors, break bread and make 0% loans to local farmers and food entrepreneurs, for the good of all. In this time of fake news and fake food, it's nice to have something real to do with our money.

Sincerely,

Woody

Woody Tasch
Founder, Slow Money Institute

" I am excited to be a founding member of SOIL. What holds more promise, on so many levels, than putting carbon back into the soil, improving access to healthy food and joyfully collaborating to rebuild community?"

—Amy Divine, Private Investor

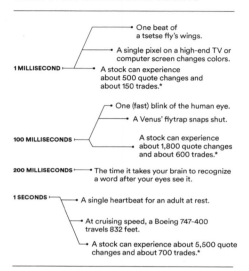

WHEN EVERY MILLISECOND COUNTS

1 MILLISECOND
- One beat of a tsetse fly's wings.
- A single pixel on a high-end TV or computer screen changes colors.
- A stock can experience about 500 quote changes and about 150 trades.*

100 MILLISECONDS
- One (fast) blink of the human eye.
- A Venus' flytrap snaps shut.
- A stock can experience about 1,800 quote changes and about 600 trades.*

200 MILLISECONDS
- The time it takes your brain to recognize a word after your eyes see it.

1 SECONDS
- A single heartbeat for an adult at rest.
- At cruising speed, a Boeing 747-400 travels 832 feet.
- A stock can experience about 5,500 quote changes and about 700 trades.*

*These are rounded numbers for actual stock symbols at their most-active period on Dec. 19, 2013, according to IEX.

New York Times Magazine, March 30, 2014

The contrast between the approach taken by SOIL and the dominant paradigm of global finance could not be clearer—although *clearer* may not be the first adjective that some would use to describe a blurring of the lines between investing and philanthropy with a combination of donations, 0% loans, collaborative decision-making, one person/one vote (no matter the size of a person's donation), and slow growth. A glance at the chart "When Every Millisecond Counts" (see margin) might snap things into sharper focus, providing a kind of exclamation point on the central importance of slow.

It is hard not to imagine that the pendulum of finance has swung too far towards ultra-fast trading and financial cleverness, too far away from people and the places where we live.

You don't have to be a Thoreauvian fiduciary activist to think back to French Prime Minister Georges Clemenceau's fateful remark during World War I, "War is too important to be left to the generals," and to wonder whether finance has become too important to be left to the financiers.

* * * * *

So, we embrace the task of bringing some of our money back down to earth.

We may be forgiven for wondering whether investing in organic farms and food businesses here in Boulder County is an exercise that is fatally tainted by elitism. Or, short of that, an ineffectual exercise, a job for the Department of Redundancy Department. After all, Boulder is a well-known hotbed of organic food entrepreneurship, the birthplace of such leading natural food companies as Celestial Seasonings and WhiteWave, and home to New Hope Network (host of the Natural Products Expos, the world's largest natural foods conventions). Boulder's place in the rarefied air of "foodie capitals" is also reflected in the fact that we are home to one of Whole Foods' top stores, with 70,000 square feet and some $70 million in sales. Across the street from this store, Google is building a new office building—which has nothing to do with food but quite a lot to do with Boulder as an elite locale. Boulder's Pearl Street sported a Tesla showroom for a few years.

On February 4, 2017, the *New York Times* ran an article in its Business Section titled "Foodies Know: Boulder Has Become a Hub for New Producers," highlighting a number of food start-ups, as well as the nonprofit support organization Naturally Boulder and investment firms Boulder Food Group and Greenmont Capital Partners:

Food and beverage start-ups in Boulder, which has just over 100,000 residents, attracted $76 million from September 2012 to September 2016, according to CB Insights, a research firm, compared with $315 million in New York and $616 million in Silicon Valley. But the vast majority of the money in New York and Northern California has gone to just a few companies. In Boulder, the money is more widely spread among dozens of companies that make everything from gluten-free cereals to probiotic drinks.

It's easy to caricature our small city as an affluent, mostly white, college town, home to gluten-free, marathon-running, rock-climbing foodies, trustafarians, Buddhists, progressives, venture capitalists, and techies. (OK, did I fail to annoy anyone?) It's also the case that the words *money* and *local food systems* conjure up, no matter what the locale, people with funds to invest and food that is not accessible to most of the population.

Boulder is a uniquely tricky place to run small, slow, and local up the flagpole. The robust start-up food scene here revolves around brands—Izze, Justin's, Boulder Brands (Evol, Earth Balance, Glutino, Smart Balance, Udi's), Boulder Organic, Rudi's Organic Bakery, Crunchsters, GoodBelly, Bobo's Oat Bars, Noosa Yoghurt, Bhakti Chai, 1908 Brands, and many more. National brands are stories, and those stories typically have little to do with place, even when they contain place names in the brand. Brands face away from place and towards markets. Could a new generation of food brands integrate into their corporate philanthropy support for local food systems? Hold that thought.

Certain aspects of the task of building local food systems here are uniquely Boulderesque, moving back and forth between progressive self-awareness and the imperatives of venture capital. At the same time, awareness of local food systems in Boulder is tied to the same systemic problems that are challenging communities across the nation—climate change and climate change denial, tribal antagonisms, elitism vs. anti-intellectualism, wealth inequality, and epic abundance alongside epidemic insufficiency.

Strolling through the farmers market along Boulder Creek on a summer Saturday morning, such systemic challenges recede from view, but they are still here, in the background, in the field of our intentions, as stubborn as weed seeds.

* * * * *

Some of us shop at the farmers market. Sixty-seven local growers participate in the Boulder Farmers Market, which attracts 250,000 visitors over its eight-month season. This is a growers-only market, meaning that it's real farmers selling the food they grow and only the food they grow. "While growers-only markets are in the minority in terms of farmers markets across the country, they offer the opportunity to connect directly with the people who grow our food and this makes them immensely valuable. It's the strength of the connection with the grower that yields the most benefits from our local food system," states Brian Coppom, Executive Director of Boulder County Farmers Markets. The Boulder market was established with seven farmers in 1987. For the past four years, sales of farm goods have been increasing at approximately 10% a year, to $2.5 million in 2016. "We're a nonprofit," Coppom continues. "This keeps us focused on our mission of helping farmers, rather than on maximizing our profitability as a social enterprise."

Some of us join a CSA. A farm that has a community supported agriculture (CSA) sells shares of the coming year's produce to its members. "This is our 10th year offering CSA shares," says Wyatt Barnes of Red Wagon Farm. "For many people, our food is the path to cooking and healthy diet change, because they have to cook what they get from us. We have over 400 shareholders who provide us with $250,000 in share purchases every spring, which is critical up-front funding for seeds, supplies, and labor at the beginning of each season. We've never defaulted on our CSA, but the possibility of a horrible hail storm is always there, and, unlike a bank, our members are willing to share risk with us. I can't over-emphasize the importance of this shared risk."

63rd Street Farm has a CSA with 320 members, produces vegetables and meat, and offers its members community-dining opportunities at its weekly pick-ups. "Building community, as well as building soil, is a key part of being a farmer," reflects Amanda Scott. "We're wondering if a member-owned cooperative might be the next step."

Mark Guttridge of Ollin Farms, which offers a farmstand, CSA, farm dinner series, and youth classes, prizes community: "The local food movement is providing a platform for a new conversation and a new culture that is emerging—being able to relate to what's growing around you, to create sustainable relationships with your neighbors, something we've lost in the global economy. There's so much to learn from a small place and from the land."

Some of us buy local food in retail stores. Willow and Mara King, co-founders of Ozuké, makers of fermented foods and beverages at their facility in nearby Lafayette, source cabbage, beets, garlic, onions, dill, cucumbers, and plums from local organic growers. "Food is about relationships, from the sourcing of it to the enjoying of it. It's important to source from people we know and want to support." In 2016, Ozuké bought 180,000 pounds of local produce from five local farmers. "Working with investors has really brought to the fore the fact that we don't all view risk the same way," says Willow King. "There are financial risks associated with investing in and running a small business, but there are also enormous societal risks associated with industrial agriculture, climate change, and health."

McCauley Family Farm grows and sells fresh organic vegetables, and raises pastured chicken and sheep on its 40 acres in Longmont. "I'm a fungi farmer, a microbe farmer, and a grass farmer," reports Marcus McCauley. "We add value to some of our produce, making sauces and fermented products which we sell through a few retail locations. My mission in life is to heal people and the earth with delicious food. I'm encouraged by the attitudes of locals in the public and private sectors—farmers, food processors, customers, regulators—as we all come together to enrich and capture yield from this bioregional food system."

Some of us patronize farm to table restaurants. "There are three upsides to our farm to table restaurant," states Eric Skokan of Black Cat Farm Table Bistro and Bramble & Hare. Eric and his wife, Jill, farm 130 acres, growing 200 vegetable varieties, and raising heritage hogs and sheep, which puts them in the unusual position of providing food directly to their own restaurant. "The first upside is personal. By integrating our farm and restaurant, I can sleep well at night, knowing that I've done everything I can to insure the integrity of the food that I serve. I am in control of the creative process, from choosing the seeds to presenting the food on the plate. The next upside is local—my participation in the Boulder community's efforts to preserve the environment and make healthy, local food accessible. The final upside is more global. The price of food on our menu includes all of the so-called 'externalities' that were required to grow our food in a healthy way. This is very important in a world where too often food purveyors do not take direct responsibility for the social and environmental costs of food production."

River and Woods restaurant was opened in 2016 by food entrepreneur Josh Dinar and Chef Daniel Asher, who has an endless, obsessive drive towards local and sustainable sourcing. Observes Asher, "The closer people are to the soil in which their food is lovingly grown, the more they will be nourished by food dense with micronutrients. This isn't just about food, however, it's about deeper connections to the land and our local community. Few things bring me greater joy than serving quality local produce to my guests. But I do bump into local supply limits along the way, including organic chicken, pastured eggs, and pastured beef."

Christine Ruch opened Fresh Thymes Eatery in 2013 with support from her customers. "We utilized a Community Supported Restaurant model," she reports. "I never could have imagined how successful this strategy would prove. Today, we have 120 members who pre-purchase $50,000 a year. At Fresh Thymes, we don't use any gluten, any primary allergens, any industrial seed oils, any sugar, any refined salt to serve delicious, local food at an affordable price."

The Kitchen's Kimbal Musk, recently featured on CNBC, has bigger plans. "Industrial food has totally failed America," said Musk, who aims to open 50 new restaurants around the country by 2020. The flagship Kitchen in Boulder sources whole cows from Colorado farms. "My brother told me it was crazy to get into the food business. I told him it was crazy to get into the space business."

Some of us donate to or participate in the programs of NGOs in the area that are working on a range of food and farming issues—groups like Growing Gardens, Chef Ann Foundation, Re:Vision, Slow Food, Hazon, Food Democracy Now, Savory Institute, and others. "Our mission is to facilitate the large-scale restoration of the world's grasslands," remarks Daniela Ibarra-Howell, CEO of Boulder-based Savory Institute. "Even though our work is global in nature, we are strongly aligned with Slow Money in that all our efforts are deployed locally, honoring context. In partnership with our network of Hubs worldwide, whence holistic land and livestock management practices are spread among pastoralists in their unique contexts, we are focused on reversing desertification, building soil carbon and fertility, and increasing awareness of the centrality of soil health for climate, food, and water security."

"The Chef Ann Foundation works with schools across the country to help them move from processed heat-and-serve to a cook-from-scratch production model," states CEO Mara Fleishman. "To date, the Chef Ann Foundation is impacting over 2.8 million kids in over 8,000 schools nationwide."

Some of us support political campaigns in hopes of influencing state and federal food and farming policy. Congressman Jared Polis, who represents the 2nd District of Colorado, was co-sponsor of federal legislation requiring the labeling of genetically modified foods.

And then comes the use of our investment capital. After our engagement as consumers, donors, and political contributors comes our engagement as investors. To address the structural problems of industrial agriculture and industrial finance, we need to bring some of our investment capital to the local table.

* * * * *

A little loosely-remembered Woody Allen from *Annie Hall* may come in handy:

> "He's depressed," Alvy's mother tells the doctor. "He won't do his homework!"

> "Is that true, Alvy?" the unctuous doctor asks, leaning towards Alvy in a patronizing manner. "Why won't you do your homework?"

> "What's the point?" the little kid with oversized spectacles replies. "The universe is expanding!"

> To which his exasperated mother retorts, "What's that got to do with anything? Brooklyn isn't expanding!"

Boulder isn't expanding, but our economy is. Today's population is 107,000, with 60,000 people commuting to Boulder daily for work; in 1990, the population was 86,000. The municipality has been more proactive than most in managing growth. In 1967, Boulder was the first city in the nation to institute a dedicated sales tax to purchase open space lands; today, the City of Boulder and Boulder County own, or have protected with easements, a total of 150,000 acres of open space, 39,000 of which are leased to farmers. As of 2015, 2,416 acres (21 farms) were organic or in transition to organic—a ten times acreage increase from 2007, with a stated county goal of 25% of leased farmland being organic by 2020.

*   *   *   *   *

The Agricultural Resources Division 2015 Annual Report, published by Boulder County Parks and Open Space, reported the results of pesticide residue testing on five farms. Below are the results of the testing, although the report did not provide guidance by which the layperson might interpret the significance of the amounts detected. (See chart on next page.)

AGRICULTURAL RESOURCES DIVISION
SOIL PESTICIDE TESTING

Ertl	Pesticide	Concentration Found
Dichlobenil	herbicide	0.017 mg/kg
p,p-DDE	insecticide	0.012mg/kg
Propiconazole	fungicide	0.016 mg/kg
Clothianidin	insecticide	0.011 mg/kg
AMPA	herbicide	0.180 mg/kg
Glyphosate	herbicide	0.078 mg/kg

Ludlow	Pesticide	Concentration Found
Dichlobenil	herbicide	0.015 mg/kg
Propiconazole	fungicide	0.032 mg/kg
AMPA	herbicide	0.150 mg/kg
Glyphosate	herbicide	0.030 mg/kg

Macy	Pesticide	Concentration Found
Dichlobenil	herbicide	0.011 mg/kg
Dieldrin	insecticide	0.0075 mg/kg
Propiconazole	fungicide	0.015 mg/kg
AMPA	herbicide	0.200 mg/kg
Glyphosate	herbicide	0.018 mg/kg

Montgomery	Pesticide	Concentration Found
Dichlobenil	herbicide	0.023 mg/kg
AMPA	herbicide	0.020 mg/kg

Strawberry	Pesticide	Concentration Found
Dichlobenil	herbicide	0.019 mg/kg
AMPA	herbicide	0.023 mg/kg

The aforementioned comment about lack of guidance with respect to the significance of detected pesticide residue was not meant to be snarky, but it does highlight how early we all are in our understanding and public discussion of many agricultural issues. It is a very good thing that the county conducts these tests and that the results are transparently reported to the public. With respect to AMPA, the report stated, "Glyphosate is degraded to AMPA (aminomethylphosphonic acid) by soil microbes." "Then what happens?" the curious nurture capitalist cannot help but ask. A subject for future consideration.

On eight Boulder County farms, average soil organic matter was estimated to be between 2 and 2.5%, and earthworm population ranged from 0 to 24 per square foot. There is no interpretive analysis of these data points and no specified county growth targets reported for either. But, as with the above, it is heartening to see initial measurements of this kind in the public square.

The Local Food Initiatives section at the report's conclusion states, "Parks and Open Space worked with Rudi's Bakery and tenant wheat farmers to explore whether locally grown wheat could be used in their bread products. A number of limiting factors were identified such as low protein content in area wheat. Rudi's subsequent sale to New York-based Hain Celestial has slowed these discussions."

* * * * *

Part and parcel of Boulder's leasing of farmland is the GMO debate, which has been raging here, as elsewhere around the country. On April 13, 2017, the Boulder County Commissioners voted 2 to 1 to proceed with a plan to phase out GMO corn and sugar beets on county land by the end of 2019 and 2021, respectively. Two documents capture the essence of this debate.

The first is the following letter from an earlier round of debate:

GMO CROPS ON BOULDER COUNTY OPEN SPACE

Letter to the Editor
Naturally Boulder Board of Directors
re: GMO crops on Boulder County Open Space

August 30, 2011

Naturally Boulder: Say NO to GMOs on Boulder County Open Space

As representatives of the local natural and organic foods community, the Naturally Boulder Board of Directors urges our Boulder County Commissioners to vote NO for GMOs on Boulder County Open Space.

While genetically modified organisms (GMOs) are not allowed in organics, not all of Naturally Boulder's membership consists of organic companies.

The pervasive nature of GMOs on U.S. farmland—be it through planting of GMO seed or GMO drift that contaminates neighboring fields—has translated into 93% of all soy and 86% of all corn grown in the U.S. now being GMO. Additionally, currently 95% of all sugar beets grown in the U.S. are GMO, and sugar beets make up approximately 55% of all sugar produced in this country. This leaves our industry with very few choices for unadulterated soy, sugar and corn-derived ingredients, such as oils used in many product formulations, should our food manufacturers choose to avoid GMOs. Additionally, as our consumers demand more environmentally friendly packaging, one of the clear leaders is PLA—compostable package made from corn—but that, too, is made from GMO corn due to the lack of availability and high price of non-GMO corn.

We have already started to see choices for better products and better packaging shrink due to GMOs in the food chain, and there are several more GMO-approved crops, such as alfalfa, that have yet to flood the market like corn and soy have. Genetically modified seeds have not been in production long enough to determine their safety, and several studies point to environmental perils related to the planting of GMO crops.

As an industry, we benefit from the Boulder brand, which stands for a healthy lifestyle, the epicenter for organic and natural foods, and a leader in environmental consciousness. Boulder residents came here to provide a better, healthier life for their families and their future. At Naturally Boulder, we nurture the Boulder brand and we believe that Boulder County must uphold the promise of Boulder in the decisions it makes today that will affect us all into the future. So, we urge our Commissioners to vote NO for GMOs on Open Space, and we urge everyone to have your voices heard before it is too late. Go to www.no-gmo-boulder.com to learn how.

Sincerely,

The Naturally Boulder Board of Directors

The second is Shay Castle's 2016 article, "Boulder County's policy for GMO on open-space farms up for renewal" from the *Daily Camera*, excerpted here:

Under a 2011 agreement with area farmers and the county, more than 1,000 of those acres are being used to grow genetically modified sugar beets and corn made to be used with the pesticide Roundup. But that could soon change.

The 2011 cropland policy is up for renewal, and if history is any indication, it will be a fierce fight. Farmers want to expand the list of allowable GMO crops, while anti-GMO activists want to see GMO crops banned entirely from open space lands [...]

A 10-hour public hearing is planned Feb. 29 to hear from groups on both sides. More than 100 people have signed up to speak, and more than 50 written comments have been received.

Traditional battle lines have been drawn, with all parties claiming to have science and ethics on their side.

A vote by the county's three commissioners later this year could further one of two visions: a Boulder County populated by dozens of small, organic farmers driving sustainable agri-tourism, or a Boulder County moving to the forefront of science and technology in agriculture, feeding the world while using fewer of its precious resources.

You can almost hear the reporter mulling the words Luddite and elitist.

* * * * *

The choice between agri-tourism and feeding the world is a false one, an ideologically driven one. There is a third way and that third way is local food systems. Such systems are not replacements for global markets and complex supply chains, but, rather, much-needed complements.

The economic, social, and environmental benefits generated by organic farming and healthy local food systems are many. The multiplier effect of dollars circulating locally. Jobs. Tax revenue. More carbon in the soil and less in the atmosphere. Less soil erosion and chemical run-off. More water in aquifers. More fresh food in schools. Trust. Conviviality. Greater community resilience in a world of increasing volatility and uncertainty.

Can we feed the world this way? Wrong question. Before we get to more useful questions, we need to reframe this issue with three data points:

— Some 40% or more of food that is grown does not make it to the consumer; there are massive amounts of food waste all along the food supply chain, from field to dumpster.

— 75% or more of the corn grown in the U.S. goes to cows and cars, and a sizeable portion of the remainder is made into high fructose corn syrup; that is, a small fraction of our corn is utilized with optimal efficiency in terms of direct human consumption.

— In terms of the volume of foodstuffs produced per acre of land, small diversified farms can out-produce large scale industrial farms by a considerable margin, but they require much more labor per acre.

It's not just a matter of producing more food for a growing population, it's a matter of *what kind of food* with which we are going to feed the world. Think: diabetes, obesity, and antibiotic use in confined animal feeding operations, just to take a few of the most obvious health and nutrition questions that cast a shadow on industrial food systems. There are many others.

So, the question of feeding the world must be deconstructed and put in a larger social and environmental context.

At the individual farm level, questions of scale and productivity are easier to see. If your goal as a farmer is to minimize labor costs and maximize acreage under production, then industrial monoculture practices are the way to go, and you'll shoot for, say, revenues of $500 per acre from thousands of acres of conventional corn. If your goal is to build soil carbon, promote biodiversity, and minimize the use of synthetic fertilizers, herbicides, and pesticides, then organic farming is the way to go, and you might shoot for, say, $20,000 per acre revenue from 20 acres of diversified vegetables and some livestock.

At the community level, we can ask a different question: Which would we like to see—more large, conventional farms or more small and mid-size farms that are as diversified and organic as possible?

My answer to this question is both agricultural and cultural:

> *For the sake of health and affection, we need more organic farms*
> *in our community and more poetry in our lives.*

* * * * *

We must remind ourselves continually that this is not an either/or choice. This is a matter of balance. Virtually all of our eggs as consumers—let's say, 96% to 98% of them, that being the amount of the food we eat that isn't produced locally—are in the basket of industrialization and globalization. The percentages are even more skewed when it comes to our eggs as investors. Virtually all of our financial eggs are in the basket of institutions that are Too Big to Fail, markets that render places invisible, and algorithms that befuddle the best and the brightest.

Those of us who want to see more small and mid-size organic producers and the local food enterprises that bring their produce to Main Street need to turn our attention away from ideological arguments about free markets or impending collapse and towards the business of putting our money to work here.

* * * * *

Boulder resident Michael Brownlee, founder of Local Food Catalysts, has been hard at it for years, building community awareness about the importance of local food systems, hosting public meetings, organizing a Slow Money investment club, stewarding a number of local investments and, most recently, organizing an online Local Food Summit. "Farmers, chefs, eaters, and food entrepreneurs across the continent are restoring soil, redefining nourishment, and reinventing business and investment models," Brownlee writes.[6] In 2012, he commissioned economist Michael Shuman to measure the impact of a shift to local food production in Boulder. The opening of that report captures the gestalt of the broader local food movement:

> Any doubts about the importance of the local food movement in the United States were dispelled in May 2007, when the cover of TIME magazine proclaimed "Forget Organic, Eat Local." That same year, the Oxford Dictionary called "locavore" one of its important new "words of the year." And Barbara Kingsolver's book *Animal, Vegetable, Miracle,* describing her family's efforts to embrace a 100-mile diet, became a national bestseller. Today, anyone who walks through an American city, suburb, or town will find at least one restaurant, supermarket, or farmers market advertising its connection to local food. Even the U.S. Department of Agriculture is celebrating and promoting local food. And the movement is spreading worldwide. Slow Food International, for example, boasts more than 100,000 members in 132 countries.

> The local food revolution has come to Boulder County, as is evident in the proliferation and success of farmers markets, community-supported agriculture (CSA) networks, restaurants and grocery stores specializing in local food, new local food delivery businesses, farm-to-school programs, and local organic food

6   "Localizing our food supply is right at the heart of a vast and spontaneous bottom-up effort to bring healing, restoration, and regeneration to our troubled world, to begin to reverse the widespread destruction caused by the industrial growth society—including by sequestering carbon and mitigating the impacts of climate change. Since food is what catalyzed human civilization in the first place, it is only appropriate that our efforts to begin healing and regeneration should also begin with food." *The Local Food Revolution: How Humanity Will Feed Itself In Uncertain Times,* Michael Brownlee (North Atlantic Books, 2016) p. 11

standards—some of which have inspired similar initiatives around the country. Many county residents, however, do not yet recognize the full significance of this revolution. They appreciate that local food is aesthetically pleasing, tastes good, and supports the growth of enjoyable farmers markets. However, many believe that local food is a luxury that's too expensive for residents living on tight budgets.

In fact, local food is becoming a powerful economic development strategy, its players in the many thousands, and its products and services increasingly competitive.

The study reports that in 2007, 746 Boulder County farms were managing 137,668 acres, including 26,451 acres of hay, 4,620 acres of wheat, 2,499 acres of corn, and 1,337 acres of barley. The total value of agricultural products sold was $34 million, with the vast majority of products exported from the county. Boulder County consumers spend $840 million per year on food—$477 million on store-bought food and $363 million on eating out. The Shuman study suggests that if 25% of the food consumed in Boulder County were produced in Boulder County, this shift would create 1,899 jobs, increasing county wages by $81 million, gross county product by $138 million, and state and local taxes by $12 million. This shift would demand 435 more people working as farmers, 350 more people in food manufacturing, and 54 more people in food service.[7]

* * * * *

Nationwide, there were 8,268 farmers markets in 2014, almost twice as many as there were in 2006. While the great recession caused direct farmer-to-consumer sales to plateau from 2007–2012, in the ten preceding years they had increased almost 70%. In 2015, organic food sales hit a new record, $43.3 billion, an increase of 11% over the preceding year. Local food sales in the U.S. grew from $5 billion in 2008 to approximately $12 billion in 2015. There were 7,398 CSAs in the U.S. in 2015, up from 60 in 1990. "Local food is rapidly growing from a niche market to an integrated system recognized for its economic boost to communities across the country," stated former U.S. Secretary of Agriculture Tom Vilsack. Boulder County is home to a few dozen CSAs with a few thousand members.[8]

Integral to such mapping of trends in organics and local food is the question of price. How much more expensive is local, organic food than the alternative? Of course, local, organic food is going to cost more than food that is produced conventionally, since the latter is the result of hundreds of years of industrialization, including large-scale monoculture, factory farms, federal commodity subsidies, and the

7   Boulder County's Comprehensive Plan acknowledges the importance of local food: "A strong local food system can positively impact the resiliency, health, economy and environment of the Boulder Valley and surrounding region. Food choices and their method of production represent one of the most significant impacts that humans have on the world around us. Sustainable agricultural practices and short distances to transport food can help reduce energy used to feed the community. Access to safe food, including locally grown food for all Boulder residents is a top priority for our community. It is important that healthy food be available to individuals and families in all neighborhoods, regardless of economic situation and location. Roots in progressive food movements run deep in Boulder County and have contributed to the dynamic and thriving natural foods industry. Many local restaurants specialize in providing local ingredients in their food, garden to table processes have been developed in local schools, and the desire for a year-round farmers market are all indications of people's growing interest and demand for locally produced food."

8   A handful of CSAs around the country have grown to more than 1,000 shares. Full Belly Farm, in the Capay Valley between San Francisco and Sacramento, has 1,200 members. Angelic Organics, which has 1,600 members in the Chicago environs, was featured in the movie *The Real Dirt On Farmer John*. On Long Island, New York, 2,100 members enjoy shares from Golden Earthworm Organic Farm.

substitution of fossil fuel for labor. All of this could be summarized as a focus on short-term productivity over long-term fertility and health. Cheap, industrially-produced food is more egalitarian in the short-term, but it degrades health and increases inequality in the long-term, driving prices down to the farmer, reducing the nutrient density of food, consolidating agriculture in the hands of large-scale producers and multinational processors, distributors and brands, and, therefore, having uneven impacts on wealth inequality and community health.

Rather than having a narrow argument about the price of a pound of organic vegetables at a farm stand versus at the supermarket, we might discuss more broadly why, for example, Italians spend 15% of their household budget on food while Americans spend less than 7%. Are Italians stupid? Constitutionally incapable of taking advantage of the efficiencies of modern agriculture and food technology? Or do they value food differently? Are they worse off, as a culture, as a people, because they spend more on food and less on other consumer goods?

Budget questions are ultimately questions of personal and political priorities. They are not fully answerable *within* economics, but include factors and values from *beyond* economics, which is why E.F. Schumacher called for meta-economic thinking. Why more aircraft carriers instead of more school lunches serving butter from 100% grass-fed cows? These become imponderably complicated issues at the level of national policy and economic theory, but they translate into far simpler choices at the local level, where dozens or scores or hundreds of us can make a tangible, direct difference.

* * * * *

We keep hearing that all politics is local, but it sure doesn't seem that way. Our attention is vacuumed up ruthlessly by national politics. It seems that the greater the institutional dysfunction, the greater the systemic ecological crisis, the more we reach for big, top-down solutions, hearing all the while that bottom-up solutions are what's really needed.

The example of Copenhagen is instructive. Robert Shiller, the Nobel laureate economist who is the Shiller of the Case-Shiller Index and author of *Irrational Exuberance* (Princeton University Press, 2000), describes how citizen action in Copenhagen catalyzed a significant community shift away from automobile commuting to bicycles:

> Copenhagen has motivated half of its habitants to commute to work by bicycle every day, the Danish government says. How did that come about? A

9   "How Idealism, Expressed in Concrete
     Steps, Can Fight Climate Change," Robert
     Shiller, *New York Times*, March 27, 2015

half-century ago, the city's inhabitants were becoming almost as reliant on cars as people anywhere else. But after the oil crisis of the 1970s, the authors point out, many Copenhagen residents made a personal commitment to ride bicycles rather than drive, out of moral principle, even if that was inconvenient for them.[9]

I think back to the many jibes at Al Gore's expense over the years about his wanting to solve climate change by getting everyone to ride bikes and change their light bulbs. I also think about the decades-old cartoon from the *Wall Street Journal*, affixed to my refrigerator door with magnets and showing a man watching TV: "Today, the world economy collapsed and everyone returned to subsistence agriculture." That may be dark humor, but it is humor, and laughter—laughing at ourselves at least as much as we lash out at politicians, economists, and others whose interests are not aligned with our own—is a way to sense what lies out there and in here, behind ideological blind spots and beyond emotional barriers to individual action.

Can we reconnect by investing in and with one another? If Copenhagen can become a leader in changing local transportation patterns, can Boulder become a leader in changing local food patterns?

Shiller continues:

> Elinor Ostrom won her Nobel in economics partly for observing that communities often solve free-rider problems. She was talking generally about contained communities like Copenhagen, not global ones. Its idealism about global warming has not spread worldwide. But she argued for a polycentric approach to climate change, with actions against global warming taken not just on a global scale but on a whole array of scales, involving smaller communities as well as the entire planet.

Shifts of this kind—Copenhagen's lessening of car-dependence and Boulder's efforts to increase local food—require slowing down. Not just physically, but financially. You can't do all this and expect to make as much money as is generated by... going fast. There are different values and an entirely different calculus at work in such matters.

In a 2015 interview with TV host Charlie Rose, former *New Republic* editor Leon Wieseltier opined that many for-profit enterprises vital to the health of culture and democracy simply do not yield financial returns that are competitive with those of tech-driven finance:

You could call it patronage, you could call it citizenship, you could call it all sorts of things. The quantification and the fiscalization of the success of such enterprises does not give you an accurate picture of their importance [...] The problem with metrics and clicks and the quantitative analysis of success is that it turns leaders into followers [...] There are lots of other things to do with a person's money. You can buy Alibaba stock. But I do not believe that the role of money in our society is only to make more money.

This is pretty darned basic, but we've already seen that in today's world the simple seems complicated, while the complicated seems simple.

Here's a simple formula:

Wieseltier + Berry – Rogue Algorithm = Nurture Capital

Add to Wieseltier's insight regarding social enterprise Wendell Berry's concept of affection, remove Rogue Algorithm's mischief, and there you have it: Nurture Capital.

Nurture capital is how we prevent local from becoming parochial. We reaffirm meta-economic values. We reaffirm the value of places against the seductions of markets.[10] We allow affection to trump geopolitics and demographics. We engage as investors, becoming more complete and active agents in local economic transformation.

Investing *ourselves* is just as important as investing our dollars. Committing our time, intelligence, and imagination to public conversation and the nurturing of shared values is vital to building a healthy community. Healthy community is vital to a healthy local economy. A healthy local economy is vital to a healthy national economy and to democracy. This investment of ourselves is not a transaction cost, something to be endured, something reluctantly borne on our way to *real* investment, that is, to financial transactions; rather, it is part and parcel of a cultural shift beyond efficiency to include diversity, beyond industrial systems to include affection. When we invest ourselves and some of our money in a local, organic food enterprise, we are completing a circle that very badly needs to be completed. For those of us engaged in this activity, this sense of completion is palpable.

Farm-to-table pioneer Odessa Piper put it best: "Local is the distance the heart can travel."

* * * * *

10   Not all communities are place-based, although it is place that is central to our discussion. Shiller also presents communities of interest as a complementary force for social change: "There are communities based on shared interests, not on geography, and people who believe in socially responsible investing may be considered one such community. If ethical investing takes the form of investing only in 'green' companies, for example, excluding companies that pollute the atmosphere, such measures may have a similar positive impact. Of course, one might dismiss ethical investing as achieving nothing more than creating opportunities for unethical investors, who will be more than happy to step in if there is money to be made. But placing a deviant enterprise on a list of companies to be avoided by ethical investors could change the moral atmosphere, much as bicycling has in Copenhagen—increasing the likelihood of a broader, successful social movement against pollution of the world's atmosphere." (Shiller, *New York Times*, March 27, 2015)

Now, I'm not going to try to convince you that with every organic beet that Anne Cure and Wyatt Barnes grow, they are bringing down the level of political rancor in this country. Or that Walt Pounds is a local economic hero. (You'll meet Walt in a minute.) Or that Willow and Mara King think that being probiotic pickleteers is somehow going to foster the proliferation of healing microbes in the gut of Wall Street. Or that the future of our economy will be shaped not only by thousands of high-tech innovators and venture capitalists, but also by millions of local nurture capitalists, organic farmers, and food entrepreneurs. I happen to think all those things are possible, but that's not what is driving us. What's driving us is something more personal. The desire to reconnect. The desire to heal. The desire to do less harm. The desire to get a little closer to the beauty of small is beautiful. The desire, in a world that is spinning out of control, for authenticity and community.

Ready. Aim. Plant.

We don't need to know who Nicholas Georgescu-Roegen was, or how he understood the relationship of economics and entropy, or what precisely triggered the collapse of Long Term Capital in 1998, or the intricacies of the most sophisticated financial razzmatazz. We don't need to know with scientific precision which pesticide in which amounts turns which microorganisms into collateral damage. We merely need to muster the imagination to hold the day's political, economic, and ideological mumbo jumbo at arm's length. We need to have enough emotional and intellectual bandwidth to hold big problems in our general awareness, while focusing on, and undertaking, small actions.

Is this a daunting challenge, an enormous opportunity, or, merely a good-old-fashioned chore? We could all use a good chore or two, couldn't we? Chores. Things we simply accept as our responsibility and take satisfaction in doing. Which could be the end of the story, except it isn't. Because beyond the chores is a new story. (And the occasional poem.) A story about life after fast food and fast money. A story about stale ideologies put aside. A call to farms.

Non-fake truth be told, they're not all that hard, these chores. For many, many rational, crazy, 19th and 20th century reasons, the work we non-farmers, we non-entrepreneurs now have before us seems daunting, but it is not. It requires only some gumption, a little money, a few hours now and again, and a few dollops of patience and care. (Oh, and did I mention the raised glasses, the bread broken, and the provender from your favorite farm?)

Ready. Aim. Plant.

The concluding two paragraphs of Christopher Alexander's four-volume, 2,165-page magnum opus, *The Nature of Order,* describe a man standing in one of Europe's great cathedrals, listening to a recorded guided tour, while live organ and voice of Haydn's mass *Sanctus* pervades the cavernous space:

> This man became a symbol for me of the loss of awe and of our loss of sense. Unable to immerse himself in the thing which filled the air and surrounded us, perhaps even unaware of the beauty which surrounded him, unaware of the size and importance of the sounds he was hearing, he was more fascinated to listen to a tape-recording reeling off the dates when the cathedral was built. For a while, during the 20th century, this had become our world: a place where the difference between awe and casual interest had been sanded down to nothing.

> But I realized on that day, that this young man's behavior could summarize what my efforts as an architect have been about. All the efforts I have made have, at their heart, just this one intention: to bring back our awe [...] and to allow us to begin again to make things in the world which can intensify this awe.

A high-functioning, diversified organic farm is not a cathedral, although it does have qualities about it that some may find worthy of awe. Awe aside, a beautiful farm does inspire that most essential quality, around which we've circled many times in these pages: *affection*.

Each of us has to decide, then: Where's our affection? What's more rewarding? Squeezing profits out by selling stock before you buy it? Betting on the next billion people around the world who want to own cars and eat more meat? Speculating on which company will be the first to Mars? Or funding Eric Skokan's new greenhouse? Conserving land for urban farming? Helping Mountain Flower Goat Dairy purchase new processing equipment? Planting seeds of nurture capital?

It's time for more of us to put our hands in the soil. The actual soil and the metaphorical soil. The soil of a restorative economy—an economy built less on extraction, consumption, and wealth, and more on preservation, restoration, and health.

Ready. A

m. Plant.

Words. Numbers. And, now, portraits. A photographic introduction to a few organic farmers and restaurateurs who source therefrom. These make their home in Boulder County, but their faces are the faces of a new generation of farmers, chefs, and food entrepreneurs who are building local food systems across the land.

McCauley Family Farm

Photo by Woody Tasch

Christine Ruch
Fresh Thymes Eatery

Photo by Kirsten Boyer

Amanda and Brian Scott
63rd Street Farm

Photos by Kirsten Boyer

Mark and Kena Guttridge
Ollin Farms

Photos by Woody Tasch

Anne Cure
Cure Organic Farm

ORGANIC

STORE

Willow King, Tara Burkley, Brian Coppom
Founding members of SOIL

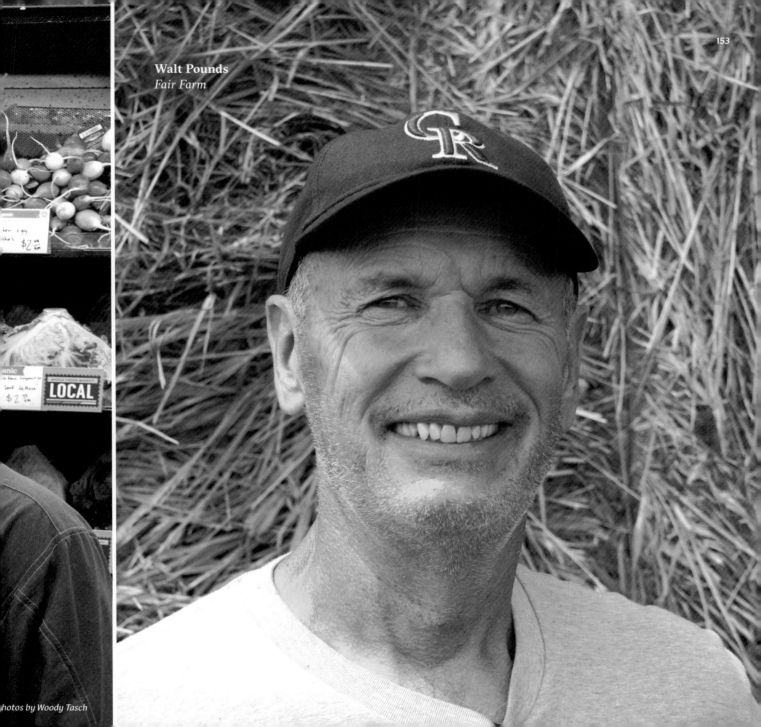

Walt Pounds
Fair Farm

LOCAL
$2

Wyatt Barnes
Red Wagon Farm

RED
WAGON
ORGANIC
FARM

Photo by Woody Tasch

RED WAGON FARM
Beets

RED WA

The Skokans
Black Cat Farm &
Black Cat Farm Table Bistro

Photos by Kirsten Boyer

Daniel Asher
River and Woods restaurant

Lyle Davis and Jesus Sanchez
Pastures of Plenty

John Ellis
Farmer John's

Afterword

Nurture and affection all around, given and received.

To and from local slow money leaders, who invest themselves so graciously in the process of bringing money back down to earth. To and from board members and kitchen cabineteers, whose collaborative spirit is beautiful. To generous donors and investors, large and small... but especially small.

Because we're all small.

When those fateful words were uttered—*small is beautiful*—a window was opened through which we have only begun to cast a few earnest, playful, sideways, inviting, mischievous, convivial, curious, lively-serious, diversity-loving, return-agnostic, chore-non-averse, beet-roasting, coquettish, roguish, meta-algorithmic glances.

History is daunting. Culture is precious. Beauty is urgent.

And Nonviolence is just over the horizon, prepping a feast for a few billion of our closest friends.

This book is printed with 70% vegetable-based inks on 100% post-consumer recycled paper. Compared to using a conventional paper stock made from virgin fiber, the first printing of the book saves the following resources:

22,652	pounds of wood *(73 average-size trees)*
34,035	gallons of water *(5½ years of daily showers)*
2,278	pounds of solid waste *(227 ten-gallon trash cans)*
6,275	pounds of CO_2 emissions *(3,337 pounds of coal burned)*